INNOVATIVE EMPLOYEE COMMUNICATION

New Approaches to Improving Trust, Teamwork and Performance

Alvie L. Smith

Prentice Hall, Englewood Cliffs, New Jersey 07632

Library of Congress Cataloging-in-Publication Data

Smith, Alvie L.
    Innovative employee communication : new approaches to improving
trust, teamwork, and performance / Alvie L. Smith.
        p.   cm.
    Includes bibliographical references and index.
    ISBN 0-13-640574-6
    1. Communication in management--United States.   2. Communication
in management--United States--Case studies.   I. Title.
HD30.3.S574   1990
658.4'5--dc20   90-40756
                                                              CIP

Editorial/production supervision
    and interior design: Elaine Lynch
Manufacturing buyer: Kelly Behr
Cover design: Lundgren Graphics

Published by Prentice-Hall, Inc.
A Division of Simon & Schuster
Englewood Cliffs, New Jersey 07632

Printed in the United States of America
10 9 8 7 6 5 4 3 2 1

ISBN 0-13-640574-6

Prentice-Hall International (UK) Limited, *London*
Prentice-Hall of Australia Pty. Limited, *Sydney*
Prentice-Hall Canada Inc., *Toronto*
Prentice-Hall Hispanoamericana, S.A., *Mexico*
Prentice-Hall of India Private Limited, *New Delhi*
Prentice-Hall of Japan, Inc., *Tokyo*
Simon & Schuster Asia Pte. Ltd., *Singapore*
Editora Prentice-Hall do Brasil, Ltda., *Rio de Janeiro*

Contents

Recent Changes in Society and the Work Place, New Human Values in the Work Place, Autocratic Managers An Endangered Species?, Role of Communication, Rights of Employees for Information, Good Communication Is Good Business, Communication As a Key Leadership Resource, Need for Dramatic Changes in American Industry, People Power and Its Proper Use, Commitment and Loyalty Can't be Mandated, Japanese Transplants Shake Up Detroit, Change Is Difficult, Agonies for Top-Level Management Too, The Pain of Change, Communication as a Change Agent

"Soul" Is Management's Attitude of Mind, Communication on the Front Lines, Upward Communication, IBM Led the Way in Upward Communication, Three-Way Communication, The Six Commandments of Effective Communication: (1) Employee communication is a fundamental component of the management system. (2) Commitment, participation and support by management at all levels is critical. (3) Communication must be a planned strategy involving both communication professionals and key management people. (4) All managers are the key conduits and catalysts. (5) Priority business issues should be core content of the communication program. (6) The communication system should undergo regular evaluation to prove its worth., Guidelines for Management, Competition in Communication, Helping Managers Manage Better, Biggest Payoff at Local Levels, Content Extremely Important, Principles of Good Communication, Credibility Is Critical, Other Media Supplement Face-to-Face Communication, Lack of Research Tools, Summary

Hurt Progress, Non-Communicator Personnel Executives, Labor Relations: Behind Closed Doors, Eleventh-Hour Blitzes Are the Normal Pattern, Management-Union-Employee Communication, In-Fighting Impedes Efforts to Survive, Media Relations: Power of the Press, Differences in Audiences, Emphasis on Long-Range, Proactive Actions, Greater Attention to Employee Interests, Tough Competing with External Media, Less In-Fighting and More Cooperation Is Needed, Securing Adequate Staff and Budget, Performance and Salesmanship, Creative Accounting, Managing Creative People, Hiring and Keeping Good Talent, Pay and Career Planning Are Important, Create Environment for Creative Thinking, Lessons Learned About Minimizing Obstacles, Summary

Cases

Preface

Employee communication (organizational communication, internal communication) is a relatively new "profession," a career field that has seen significant advances during the past two decades.

Its importance as a management resource has increased dramatically as a result of intense worldwide competition. This is particularly true as it relates to Japanese producers and their demonstrated ability to combine technical and human resources into masterly displays of industrial success. But the prospects of a super European economic community and expanded consumer demand in Russia and China add further dynamics to the world competitive environment.

The challenge for global economic leadership has been issued and the race is on—with incredible rewards to the winners.

This book discusses how internal communication can play a critical role in bringing employees into a more understanding, cooperative and productive relationship with management, while at the same time improving their satisfaction and quality of life at work. Although the book's major emphasis is on the industrial sector, the principles and examples of sound communication it discusses have application to virtually all organizations—including private and public, profit and nonprofit, large and small.

In many businesses today, there is a strong undercurrent of anger, resentment, fear and mistrust among employees, directed against almost invisible managements. The warm, personal "family" business environments of a generation or so ago have been replaced by a lack of understanding among employees about what's going on. There is a feeling of hopelessness about their own job destinies and a lack of confidence in management which doesn't really seem to be concerned about their personal welfare.

"DECADE OF THE EMPLOYEE"

The 1980s was a decade of greatly increased efforts by corporate communicators to improve on-going communication with external audiences. The goal was to enhance sales and corporate image, and the primary targets were stockholders, the financial community, customers and, to a significant degree, the general public. In the process, most companies ignored or took for granted their most critical constituency—their employees.

But increasing competitive pressures have made it very clear that the 1990s will be the decade of the employee. And winning back the loyalty and commitment of employees will be the greatest challenge facing corporate communicators in this decade.

Some experts believe that what is needed could be a very simple formula for a new work environment. This formula would be founded on simple, honest principles of human relations. These would include sharing, trust, concern and respect for the individual, participative management, teamwork, commitment, receptivity to new ideas, fair incentives and a sincere interest in employees as persons as well as workers.

But converting that formula to actuality is extremely difficult because of the entrenchment of traditional autocratic management systems in major American institutions. The key is a basic change in management attitudes, one that sees two-way communication not as a bothersome chore but as a fundamental means of helping to release the creative genius which is bottled up in organizations by authoritarian management styles.

IN THE FRAMEWORK OF ENLIGHTENED MANAGEMENT

Helping to facilitate that change in management attitudes and actions represents a formidable assignment. It will take the best talents of the communicator, relying not only on experience and training but also on the power of innovative thinking, to help forge a more productive, respectful partnership between management and employees.

That's the framework of enlightened management in which this book is created.

Associates have asked if the book is based largely on the experiences of General Motors. The answer is yes and no.

Auto analyst Maryann Keller says in *Rude Awakening:*

> GM of the 80s is the story of a company that recognized it needed to change, but found itself hopelessly tangled in a complex corporate culture which resisted change...GM's struggle during the past 10 years says a lot about who we are as a people...[and GM's] prospects for the future are a reflection of where our nation is going...GM is not an abstract reality for any person in America. It is everything about our country we are proud of and everything that we wrestle with.[1]

GM's agonizing challenges of the 1980s are not dissimilar to those experienced by other major U.S. companies trying to modernize basic philosophies, approaches to world markets and customers, and relationships with both employees and unions. In fact, many of the companies discussed in this book have been deeply involved in major modernization programs. The huge efforts being expended at many companies will make a significant contribution to the competitive strength of American industry.

BROAD-BASED REFLECTION OF INDUSTRIAL AMERICA

In the same way, this book discusses communication experiences of General Motors, heavily interlaced with those of nineteen other well-known U.S. companies. Employee populations in these companies range from 13,000 to 775,000. Much of the material in this book represents original reporting about the experiences of 40 communication professionals, educators and business executives from 30 organizations—material which I gathered in correspondence and interviews, either in person or by telephone. These collective experiences provide a broad-based reflection of industrial America and

[1] From *Rude Awakening: The Rise, Fall and Struggle for Recovery of General Motors* by Maryann Keller. Copyright (c) 1989 by Maryann Keller. Reprinted by permission of William Morrow & Co., pp. 11–12.

its need to strengthen global competitiveness through better use of people and the communication resource. Included as participants are:

> Allstate Insurance Company; Aluminum Company of America (ALCOA); American Telephone and Telegraph Corporation (AT&T); Atlantic Richfield Company (ARCO); Chevron Corporation; E.I. duPont de Nemours and Company (Du Pont); Federal Express Corporation (FedEx); Ford Motor Company; General Electric Company (GE); International Business Machines Corporation (IBM); Johnson & Johnson; Hewlett-Packard Company (H-P); New United Motor Manufacturing, Inc. (NUMMI); Nissan Motor Manufacturing Corporation, USA; Parker Hannifin Corporation; Union Carbide Corporation (UCC); United Technologies Corporation (UTC); Weyerhaeuser Paper Company; and Xerox Corporation. Other contributors were the consulting firm of Towers, Perrin, Forster and Crosby (TPF&C) and the Research Foundation of the International Association of Business Communicators (IABC).

No individuals are called out for criticism in the book. But there are critical observations about institutions, traditions, relationships, power and politics, and about employee loyalties, confidence, trust, fears and untapped potential—both in GM and other companies. These are fundamental to the book's primary purpose, which is to provide experience-based lessons, right and wrong, which may be useful to managers and communication practitioners.

There are footprints of people—including management at all levels—that will no doubt match those in many organizations, large and small. Many of the desires and sins of communication are universal.

By being used as the foundation for discussion of the employee communication function in a reluctant environment, GM may get more negatives than it deserves in comparison to other companies which have gone through similar problems during the past two decades. Consultant Roger D'Aprix, of William M. Mercer, Inc., perhaps put this point in proper perspective when he told a seminar at the 1987 International Association of Business Communicators in London: "GM's program is the most methodical assault on the problem of organizational communication I have ever seen."

WIDE RANGE OF SUBJECTS COVERED

Subjects to be covered in this book include:

- Basic concepts of effective communication—and how they fit into a total strategic plan.
- Building a cohesive, cooperative management network by establishing communication as a primary responsibility of every member of management.
- The importance of systematic research—to highlight deficiencies, direct improvements and provide proof of value for management.
- How the communicator can sell the program to management—not just to the chief executive officer but to the entire management group. The book stresses the critical importance of innovative approaches, which combine sound management practices with imaginative ideas to enhance the value and appeal of the total communication process.
- How to make the most effective use of all media in a diversified communication system.
- Major obstacles to effective communication—from a lack of management understanding to autocratic bureaucracies, from lack of trust to teeth-grinding politics.
- Making the most out of being creative—using innovative ideas both to stimulate interest and enthusiasm and to boost the participation and support of employees and management people, too.

DESIGNED FOR COMMUNICATORS, MANAGERS, STUDENTS

This book is designed to help professional communicators and work managers in all kinds of organizations—public and private—and also to be helpful for students planning careers in this field.

For *communicators,* it offers a philosophy of modern communication, along with basic concepts, ideas and techniques based on experiences from a number of companies. In encouraging communicators to think like managers, the book offers many ideas for selling their programs to managers and for working more closely with them in achieving organizational goals. It also encourages communicators to be imaginative, to move beyond safe harbors in seeking higher levels of performance and contributions.

For *managers,* it offers a valuable resource for strengthening their leadership potential through the systematic sharing of information as a means of maximizing employee understanding, trust and performance. In encouraging managers to think like communicators, it helps them understand the powerful potential of this resource in accomplishing their personal and organizational goals.

It is the combination of efforts by the manager and the professional communicator—a meeting of minds and purposes—that produces the best results and strengthens the value of communication as a management resource. This book will help managers and communicators understand this synergistic alliance and how it can be a powerful resource for them—individually, and with much greater success, as partners.

For *students,* this book can be the best of two worlds, spotlighting communication from the perspectives of both the manager and the professional communicator. It provides front-line insight into a high-potential career field—a solid foundation of experience and battle-tested case examples of how good communication can be a dynamic force for progress and change.

This is a rare opportunity to view the employee communication profession from the inside out rather than seeing it as most textbooks do—from the outside in. It is indeed "a view from the trenches."

Acknowledgments

Many people helped me with this book, most of whom are named in the text. I want to give special thanks to:

Roger Smith, former chairman of General Motors, whose long-term support began with his approval of a long-range strategic communication plan in 1975 when few other GM executives had the vision to see its value;

Tony De Lorenzo, former vice president for public relations, who adopted and nurtured the foundling program when responsibility passed from the GM personnel administration and development staff to public relations;

Jack McNulty, former GM vice president for public relations, who was a strong supporter of new and innovative ideas during the 1980s, ideas which brought the employee communication program to maturity;

Bruce McCristal, Allan Csiky and Andrea Koterba, co-architects of GM's corporate-wide system, who provided helpful criticism and guidance for the book;

Roger D'Aprix and Mike Emanuel, who as consultants helped build the GM program and contributed ideas for this book;

Bob Berzok, Brad Whitworth and Ben Thompson, who gave valuable input and support, particularly in ideas and in the sharpening of text;

Last, but certainly not least, my old mentor and long-time friend Scott Cutlip, who tore my first draft to shreds (thank God!) and provided on-going counseling which added greatly to the overall focus of the book.

I am grateful to all of these people and also to others who worked (and are still working) to incorporate into GM's management philosophy the basic principle of honest, open communication as an essential element of leadership and organizational success.

Chapter I

Introduction:
Laying the Groundwork

American companies today are fighting for their business lives, trying to regain world leadership against intensely competitive domestic and overseas manufacturers. And global competition will become even more formidable as the expanding wave of democracy opens new markets in major population areas of the world.

In recent years, it has become increasingly clear that bricks and mortar, advanced technology, outstanding products and sophisticated marketing alone cannot do the job required for world leadership. People are the big difference. And to a large degree, the big difference in people, their organizations and their competitive vitality is how well they communicate with each other.

RECENT CHANGES IN SOCIETY AND THE WORK PLACE

In the ever-changing patterns of life and work in America, effective communication between individuals—whether in giant corporations or in small groups—is a major force in ordering priorities and determining winners. The truth is that communication is such a fundamental part of managing today that without it, virtually nothing can be accomplished.

The importance of effective internal communication has been intensified because of the dramatic changes that have taken place in our society in the past 10 to 20 years. Nowhere is it more pronounced than in the business and industrial world. Unprecedented global competition has magnified the urgent need to modernize America's aged industrial facilities in order to improve both quality and productivity levels. Equally important is the need to modernize management thinking about the most productive use of people in all aspects of the business.

An avalanche of takeovers, mergers, acquisitions and downsizings has created confusion among employees about priorities, leadership and their own personal security. Employees' confidence and loyalty have turned to uncertainties, antagonism and fear about their futures.

The information explosion has brought about a critical need for more effective communication within business organizations, which have to compete with external media in spreading the message of management's goals and expectations to employees.

But changes in the human element of business and industrial environments have been equally dramatic. Employees are better educated, more sophisticated and more demanding in what they expect from their jobs. They are capable of much higher levels of contributions if only management can succeed in opening channels to their creativity, loyalty and commitment. Their contributions increase with better understanding and with actions confirming that management is sincerely receptive to their ideas and their personal aspirations.

NEW HUMAN VALUES IN THE WORK PLACE

In fact, a new set of human values is emerging in the American work place, paralleling those in society as a whole—values that translate into demands for greater democracy and a more enjoyable quality of work life. Increased employee participation, decision-making responsibilities and job satisfaction—not higher pay and benefits— are the ultimate weapons in the drive for higher levels of employee performance.

Indeed, more top business executives are beginning to say without apologies that the bottom-line goals of "people programs" are to achieve better quality, higher productivity and increased profits, while improving employee morale and satisfaction as a planned part of the whole process. More and more, employees and unions are pledging fuller cooperation to help make their companies more competitive and their jobs more secure—even though strong pockets of resistance to high levels of management-employee-union teamwork persist.

AUTOCRATIC MANAGERS AN ENDANGERED SPECIES?

In the context of a modern management philosophy, authoritarian managers are an endangered species—or certainly should be. Iron-fisted managers in most organizations are a liability and simply cannot expect maximum performance and loyalty from their employees; they are a costly management relic which most organizations can no longer afford. But the "rule-by-fear" management concept is an addiction difficult to deny and still exists in many businesses today.

The real premium need in American business is for enlightened management which inspires, stimulates and rewards employee initiative and creativity, the wellsprings of industrial progress. Employees who are treated with respect, as equals within the organization in a two-way exchange of information with management, generally will support the goals of that organization, in good times and bad.

The big payoff, of course, will come to organizations that can build a manager-employee relationship based on trust, mutual respect and confidence in what committed people can accomplish; and that can share information and power for the good of the organization and its employees.

ROLE OF COMMUNICATION

The hard realities of worldwide competition have brought a new urgency for industry to achieve leaner, more efficient business organizations and improved teamwork among employees, management and unions. And good communication is essential to the achievement of these goals.

For its part, management should not tolerate—nor should it ignore or support—the type of haphazard, reactive, afterthought, Band-Aid approaches that characterized too many employee communication programs of the past. There is no place for any management activities that do not contribute to organizational goals or legitimate employee needs—and that certainly includes internal

communication. Communication professionals must be as aggressive as accountants, engineers, and manufacturing and marketing
people in supporting operating goals in a cost-effective manner.

In short, the internal communication function should be recognized as an integral part of modern management in virtually every
organization, public and private. But to earn a lasting place at the
management table, such a program must demonstrate purpose,
continuity, credibility and value.

RIGHTS OF EMPLOYEES FOR INFORMATION

One of the toughest jobs for professional communicators is to demonstrate to managers that the act of communicating openly and
regularly with employees is not just an altruistic obligation but one
that can affect business results—in negative or positive ways. The
basic premises of this viewpoint are that

- employees at all levels have the right to expect their
  managers to include them in the basic information flow;
- they have the right to expect managers to seek their ideas
  on how to improve the business and to give these ideas
  proper consideration;
- they have the right to be treated as important, individual,
  contributing members of the team who can be trusted to
  use even sensitive information responsibly; and
- they have the right to be empowered with the highest
  possible level of responsibility for the benefit, not only of
  the organization, but also their own sense of achievement
  and job satisfaction.

Obviously, open, two-way communication is the first step in
achieving these goals.

GOOD COMMUNICATION IS GOOD BUSINESS

From the standpoint of management, it is necessary to sell it on the
principle that good communication is simply good business. This is
true because informed employees

- have a better understanding of the business and reasons
  for management actions;

- are better equipped to contribute to improved performance, both as individuals and as team members;
- can better understand and maximize their role in the company's success; and
- have a greater recognition of how their performance affects their own personal reward and security systems.

This type of enlightened partnership doesn't come about overnight. And the process must begin with a strong and repeated commitment at the highest levels that effective communication is a way of life for the entire organization.

COMMUNICATION AS A KEY LEADERSHIP RESOURCE

Scott Cutlip, Dean Emeritus of the College of Journalism and Mass Communication at the University of Georgia, is a strong supporter of effective internal communication as an integral component of leadership.

> Unfortunately, too many of our institutions, like the dinosaur, have outgrown their central nervous systems. As a result, believable messages often don't reach all parts of the organization with the speed and accuracy needed to achieve maximum performance.
>
> Communication must be viewed as the key resource of leadership. It starts with the chief executive who makes internal communication his or her first priority, both by precept and by example. But even with gung-ho support by the top bosses, many tough barriers to free-flowing communication will remain in many organizations. Conquering these obstacles requires the best talents of skilled communication professionals day in, day out.
>
> Successful attainment of organizational goals requires a free, candid flow of information among all levels and groups. It is a foolish executive who leaves internal communication to chance or to the grapevine. The goals of communication are to identify, establish and maintain mutually beneficial relationships between the organization and its employees, on whom its success or failure depends.

Basic principles of good communication, of course, are universal and have application to virtually all organizations—including manufacturing firms, government agencies, universities, churches and hospitals; and nonprofit as well as profit-oriented businesses. Specific action programs which put these principles into operation may vary, based on differing conditions at each company or location. Generally speaking, the communication task becomes more difficult as the organization grows in size and complexity and in the geographic spread of its operations.

NEED FOR DRAMATIC CHANGES IN AMERICAN INDUSTRY

There is widespread agreement that America's return to industrial world leadership depends to a major degree on how well it can improve its abilities to develop and effectively use human capabilities. It is a monumental task that—even from this point forward—will take time and involve many changes in fundamental supervisory structures, in the work environment and in management attitudes concerning the management, development and effective use of people.

> The American worker has become the victim of an industrial system that neither acknowledges, values nor profits by his or her potential.

Robert J. Stramy, one of the most successful plant managers at General Motors, says that American industry, to be globally competitive, must dramatically transform its manufacturing operations to take full advantage of the genius of its employees, as well as advances in technology. (Case Example 1 at the end of this chapter, pages 13-16, discusses Stramy's remarkable success in creating a new work environment at GM's Cadillac Engine Plant in Livonia, Michigan.)

The American worker, on the other hand, has become the victim of an industrial system that neither acknowledges, values, nor profits by his or her potential to contribute to the corporation.[1]

[1] Robert J. Stramy, John J. Nora and C. Raymond Rogers, *Transforming the Work Place* (Princeton, N.J.: Princeton Research Institute, 1986), p. 4.

While American industry focuses primarily on investment in capital equipment, Japanese companies invest simultaneously in capital equipment, state-of-the-art technology and human resources. Japanese auto workers receive five times more training per year than their American counterparts, resulting in a well-trained, committed work force, consistently involved in decision making and problem solving and directly responsible for quality and productivity.

Dick Charlton, vice president of corporate communications at Parker Hannifin, emphasizes:

[We need] more motivational programs to focus employees on continuous improvements in productivity, quality and customer service. Foreign competition—from an integrated Western Europe, perhaps from Eastern Europe, and from the surging Pacific Rim—will require superior performance from the U.S. work force if we're to survive.[2]

PEOPLE POWER AND ITS PROPER USE

The importance of "people power"—and its use—is a key subject in a major study of the communication profession being directed by Dr. James E. Grunig of the University of Maryland, and sponsored by the International Association of Business Communicators.

In discussing preliminary findings of his study group concerning what makes "excellence in organizations," Grunig says:

Excellent organizations empower people by giving employees autonomy and allowing them to make strategic decisions. They also pay attention to the personal growth and quality of work life of employees. They stress the interdependence rather than independence of employees, integration rather than segmentation, and strike a balance between teamwork and individual effort...

Excellent organizations give people power by eliminating bureaucratic, hierarchical organizational structures... They decentralize decisions, managing without managers as much as possible. They also avoid stratification of employees.[3]

---

[2]Richard G. Charlton, "The Decade of the Employee," *Public Relations Journal* (January 1990), p. 26.

[3]James E. Grunig, ed., *Excellence in Public Relations and Communication Management: Contributions to Effective Organizations* (Hillsdale, N.J.: Lawrence Erlbaum Associates, forthcoming, 1991.)

COMMITMENT AND LOYALTY CAN'T BE MANDATED

Today's employees have a lot of options, some enforced by the
unions, that they can exercise if they don't like or understand
management actions. One of the most damaging is simply to with-
hold their best efforts, ideas and suggestions, to just cruise along
with passable performances. Or simply to stay away from work as
many days as they can get away with. Multiplied among all the
members of the employee group, this negative employee option can
have a devastating effect on both quality and performance.

The annual cost of poor employee loyalty across American
businesses is probably astronomical when areas such as absenteeism, quality, productivity, employee turnover and theft are included.

Absenteeism Is A Major Competitive Factor. If you have
any doubts, look at the statistics on absenteeism in U.S. industrial
operations. Direct costs to business are estimated to be in the tens
of billions of dollars annually. And because of unauthorized absenteeism, domestic producers in the U.S. auto industry suffer multi-
billion dollar losses each year in terms of lost time, poor quality,
warranty costs, production disruptions and morale—particularly
among those who do come to work every day.

In a 1990 report evaluating auto industry competitiveness
during the 1980s, noted consultant James Harbour pointed to absenteeism as a key factor in the strong competitive advantage
Japanese transplants located in the U.S. enjoy over domestic auto
producers. Specific figures from domestic producers are very difficult to secure. But *The Harbour Report* said that absenteeism at
U.S. Japanese plants, including planned vacations and personal
time off, runs about five percent. This compares to an estimated
range of twelve to sixteen percent average occurring at GM, Ford
and Chrysler plants.[4]

That makes absenteeism a real big-ticket item, and not only in
terms of manufacturing efficiency and profits. It is also a clear
indication of the superiority of the Japanese approach to management-employee-union relations and teamwork. Absenteeism is not

[4] James Harbour, et al., *The Harbour Report: A Decade Later (Detroit, Mich.:
Harbour and Associates, Inc. 1990), pp. 213–215.*

a cause, but a symptom. It is a red flag that something is fundamentally wrong in the relationship between management and employees and in the commitment of both employees and unions for 100 percent contribution to organizational goals.

Blind loyalty of employees to their companies—as it once was— is gone forever. Commitment and loyalty can't be mandated or bought automatically with the paycheck. They have to be earned through mutual respect, understanding, partnership, caring and trust between management and employees.

Robert H. Waterman, Jr., talks about the relationship between communication and commitment in *Renewal Factor*.

> Communicate extensively to create the link between causes and the commitment individual employees make to them. You can't force people to be committed; neither can you control whether or not they stay committed.
>
> The best approach is to be the source of clear, consistent, honest information. When in doubt, tell people too much. The more they know about your cause, the more they can help in ways you wouldn't have expected. The more they find they can help, the more commitment they feel. Respect people enough to be straight with them about the down side as well as the up side; that, too, strengthens commitment.[5]

This is more critical today than ever before because of the highly competitive world markets, which not too many years ago we had almost all to ourselves. And certainly the Japanese have demonstrated how to maximize employee loyalty and performance, not only in their home plants, but also in American operations using American workers.

JAPANESE TRANSPLANTS SHAKE UP DETROIT

The importance of managing people with a more participative, decision-sharing approach was emphasized in a *Business Week* cover story entitled "Shaking Up Detroit." It highlighted the increasing threat to the domestic auto industry posed by Japanese car assembly plants in America.

[5]Robert H. Waterman, Jr., *Renewal Factor* (New York: Bantam Books, Inc., 1987), p. 309.

According to data from *Ward's Automotive Reports* (cited in the BW article), Japanese transplants, from 1984 to 1989, increased their share of all cars built in the U.S. from two percent to nearly fifteen percent and this figure is expected to rise sharply higher in the 1990s.

The *Business Week* article goes on to say:

> The Japanese invasion represents a great deal more than a marketing problem for General Motors, Ford and Chrysler. It's penetrating the very heart of the domestic industry, challenging managerial mindsets and traditional, often obsolete relations between producers and suppliers, management and labor...

> Although powerful forces within the industry are resisting change, the Big Three are slowly disassembling management and production methods and are remaking them along Japanese lines. Companies that had nearly given up on American workers are finding that giving them decision-making powers can be a powerful motivator.[6]

CHANGE IS DIFFICULT

Many managers in American industry were brought up on such need-to-know rules as "don't tell employees anything unless they need the information to do their specific jobs; it's none of their business why management shut down an operation, eliminated a product line, bought a new high-tech company or modified employee/retiree benefits."

Change is difficult for most people. In fact, resistance to change is one of the strongest laws of human nature. The greater the magnitude of change, the more severe the discomfort and reluctance of people to support the change.

Managers often fear increased employee participation because it involves sharing information and power. First-level supervisors, particularly, are concerned about further erosion or even elimination of their positions as more emphasis is placed on broader employee participation, on teamwork, on more efficient organizational structures and on increased information sharing.

[6]Robert D. Hof and James B. Treece, "Shaking Up Detroit," *Business Week* (August 14, 1989), pp. 74–76.

AGONIES FOR TOP-LEVEL MANAGEMENT TOO

To say that the massive changes taking place in many companies are traumatic is a gross understatement. And let us not forget that the reorientation of organizational structures, thinking and cultures accompanying these changes is also traumatic for top executives who are diligently, and sometimes frantically, searching for answers to propel their organizations successfully into the twenty-first century.

These are the agonies of top-level management, whose task is monumental in times of massive change. But executives should never forget that the transition will be much easier if they can persuade all employees that the eventual benefits from changes being made—with job security being a major factor—make them worth the risks and pain involved. Good communication can help to do that.

THE PAIN OF CHANGE

Mark Potts and Peter Behr, in *The Leading Edge,* talk about the pain of change and the role communication plays in helping companies, through the process of continuing change, to stay on the leading edge of competition.

> The changes needed to put American companies on the leading edge of the competitive world will not come without pain, but that pain can be minimized through sensitive management and attention to the human details. There is no way to eliminate all the human hardships of change, but the pain of not making the required corporate and management changes to adapt to the new environment is likely to be much greater...The bottom line for this worker-management partnership, then, is communications. The relationship must be built on a solid, factual understanding about the company's position...[7]

COMMUNICATION AS A CHANGE AGENT

Because of its role in explaining and stimulating discourse on the processes of change, employee communication serves as a powerful

[7]Mark Potts and Peter Behr, *The Leading Edge* (New York: McGraw-Hill Publishing Co., 1987), p. 115.

agent of change in its own right. Good communication can help ease the pain of change. It can be used to provide reasons to employees and unions (and external audiences, too), serving as a basis for understanding and acceptance even when loss of jobs is part of the bottom line.

In fact, helping to define and relate the new corporate cultures to employees on an individual and team basis has become an urgent priority for internal communicators in major American institutions. Employees need to understand the business in the context of the new culture's requirements and promise. They need to know what is expected of them and how the new levels of performance translate into meaningful work, security and advancements. Without this type of understanding, most employees will simply not be willing, or know how, to modify established attitudes and work behavior required to make change successful and personally rewarding.

The communication process must recognize other key management elements in seeking constructive change in the organizational culture—such as human relations, organizational development and strategic planning—and it must join forces with them, if possible, in peer or leadership relationships.

Outside the company's walls, management desperately needs the support of employees in defending management positions, including those affecting proposed new government regulations. And, of course, securing this type of employee support is more achievable if management has a base of credibility, a reputation for being honest with employees over time.

This is the enlightened management environment in which the employee communication process is emerging as a dynamic force—a cornerstone of any successful organization. Only time will tell how well the employee communication function performs in helping to transform corporations and other American institutions into the revitalized, more competitive organizations required for world leadership in the 1990s and beyond.

CASE 1

Cadillac Livonia Engine Plant

TEAMWORK, UNDERSTANDING
AND COMMUNICATION
PRODUCE DRAMATIC RESULTS

A revolutionary concept in organization development was launched in 1979 at the Livonia Engine Plant of the Cadillac Division of General Motors in Michigan. It was to be a state-of-the-art plant: in product and process technology and in the development of a new work environment. The goal was to open new doors of opportunity for human contributions by eliminating traditional obstacles between management, unions and employees.

Communication was the strong webbing which was to hold the experiment together, and the experiment's progress was to be demonstrated in forty different measurements for all employees to see.

TRANSFORMATION OF AMERICAN INDUSTRY

Robert J. Stramy,[*] plant manager at the time, told the story of the "Livonia Opportunity" in a book entitled *Transforming the Work Place,* which he co-authored with John J. Nora and C. Raymond Rogers.

The Livonia concept gave equal balance to product quality, productivity and quality of work life. Full management-union cooperation was essential.

---

*Stramy subsequently served as manager of GM's engine-and-car assembly plants in Saltillo, Mexico, from 1984 until mid-1988, when he became manager of GM's huge Chevrolet-Pontiac-Canada assembly plant in Van Nuys, California. In 1989, he became an executive vice president of GM Overseas Corporation and joint representative director of Daewoo Motor Company, Ltd., a GM joint-venture operation based in Seoul, South Korea.

The first paragraph in the plant's operating philosophy articulates the vision well.

Together through trust, communication and respect for the individual, we will build an organization supportive of all employees in the development and utilization of their knowledge, ability and skill towards the achievement of personal as well as organizational goals.

A special planning team was a major force. Close cooperation involving management, union and employees was essential on this team and in all phases of implementation. It took about a year to get the total program fully operational.

TEAMWORK WAS FOUNDING PRINCIPLE

The entire project was founded on the principle of teamwork—of letting all employees participate in the decision-making process. It promoted equal opportunity for all employees to contribute to and to share in the rewards of success and in the dignity of their place of work. Special dining rooms and parking spaces for managers were eliminated. White shirts and ties for supervisors were taboo.

Business teams gave greatly increased responsibilities to hourly employees. The position of general foreman was scrapped; all job designations were eliminated except for one: quality operator.

Employees were encouraged to learn as many jobs as possible, and pay was raised through a "pay-for-knowledge" system based on how many new jobs they learned. All employees were given a heavy schedule of special training to help orient them to the new environment. Team reviews and appraisals replaced the corporation's traditional superior/subordinate appraisal procedure.

PRACTICAL, RELIABLE COMMUNICATION

The plan called for practical and reliable systems of two-way communication, including:

- weekly team meetings, for one hour, on company time,
- daily meetings of the supervisory staff, with participation by the union and quality operators,
- weekly staff meetings,
- monthly meetings between the staff and team coordinators,

- a system of regular performance progress reports, and
- a weekly plant newspaper, which featured regular reports of progress, suggestions and awards.

There was a weekly report on forty key performance indicators involving product quality, productivity and industrial relations—information made available to all employees. Here are a few examples:

Productivity. The *productivity* indicator focused on average number of pieces produced and shipped per day, repair inventory, number of engines produced per employee, number of direct and indirect hours per engine, daily scrap, machine uptime, maintenance labor, and overtime and cost per unit.

Quality. The *quality* indicator dealt with a number of factors such as quality index, defects per engine, engine pulls, warranty costs, and customer satisfaction index.

Industrial Relations. This indicator dealt with absenteeism, grievances, injuries, suggestion frequency for individuals and teams, and percent of pay-for-knowledge levels attained.

Was the "Livonia Opportunity" a success? Here are just a few results after the first two years:

- There was a 100 percent increase in daily production the first year, 20 percent the second.
- Warranty claims were down 56 percent the first year, 29 percent the second.
- There was a reduction of 50 percent in controllable cost per engine.
- Scrap was reduced 37 percent.
- There was an increase of 33 percent in machine uptime.
- Absenteeism was reduced 50 percent.
- Grievances during the entire first year were equal to just one normal week's load.
- Employees contributed ten times as many suggestions as the average employee for the rest of Cadillac.

Stramy says:

It's not just sharing information—it's how you do it. You need constant emphasis with both managers and employees of how the experiment is going, and to report their contributions in a continuous improvement system. In the process, you build fires of satisfaction, a sense of belonging and personal commitment among the entire work force.

LIVONIA IS MODEL OPERATION

The Livonia plant is still recognized as one of the model production operations in General Motors, Stramy says.

> Good communication must be given a top priority in efforts to transform American industrial operations out of the past and into the 21st century. A properly designed communication system is the glue that holds the organization together in its efforts to continuously improve the quality, productivity and responsiveness necessary to satisfy today's highly demanding customers.

> Without consistent and reliable communication of progress and problems to all employees, their interest and efforts lag. And the constant sharing of ideas, problems and plant information on a face-to-face basis is the heartbeat of any process with this magnitude of change.

Chapter 2

The Six Commandments: Basic Principles of Communication

Effective employee communication programs must have both body and soul.

Most programs have basic "body components"—some good, some bad—which include things like printed materials, telephone or electronic newslines, video and film presentations and face-to-face communication in various forms. Some also have regular evaluation procedures which ensure that the communication function is alive and well—doing the job it is expected to do.

These communication activities—even if conducted in a haphazard, uncoordinated manner—will produce a warm, cozy feeling for the communicator and employees. And they will make most managers feel good, too.

Communication programs may even win awards in professional competition. Everybody can say, "See! Now we're really communicating."

But will the communication program work well in good times and bad? Will it earn respect from top executives as an essential part of the management process? Will it make a continuing contribution to bottom-line results—in both performance and employee relations? Perhaps most important, will employees believe in it?

If you answered one or more of these questions in the negative, chances are that your program—even if it has a good-looking body—doesn't have "soul." It doesn't have an inner commitment by both management and employees for open, candid communication.

"SOUL" IS MANAGEMENT'S ATTITUDE OF MIND

The "soul" of an organization's internal communication system is management's attitude of mind. This state of mind has to be part of management philosophy, one which must start with the chief executive officer and be accepted and practiced by the entire management group.

The soul gains its power from a management attitude that says communicating with your own people is essential to organizational success. The idea is to make good communication instinctive, the normal gut reaction of managers to share information, to encourage good ideas and to transmit the information they receive to other appropriate people in all directions.

The goal is not just to share information, but to build understanding and to help resolve conflicts and motivate positive actions. It works best when there is trust, a feeling of teamwork and mutual respect between managers and employees. It works worst—if at all—when the process is based on mistrust and deceit, on a ruthless exercise of authority, discipline, intimidation and fear.

Many people—including some professionals—are inclined to look at communication as a job which is handled largely through formal media. But the most effective communication is not accomplished through the use of printed materials, visuals and spoken words which originate in the employee communication office. It comes from the soul.

It is a process which has its basic foundation in the *management style* of an organization—from top to bottom and sideways too—one committed to making communication a working reality on the front lines where it counts the most.

COMMUNICATION ON THE FRONT LINES

Frank Schotters, retired plant manager of the General Motors car assembly operation in Lansing, Michigan, believes in giving employees essentially the same information as managers and trusting them to use it properly.

> There's nothing really confidential in this business if you want to bring about change—whether it's negative or positive in terms of employee jobs. You simply have to share information openly and honestly with employees on a regular basis. That's the way you earn their understanding, trust and a high level of cooperation.

> If employees are given the same information base from which management decisions are made, chances are high that they'll arrive at the same conclusion. Or at worst, they will understand the reasons for management's decision, will feel like members of the team and will work hard to make the decision successful.

UPWARD COMMUNICATION

To strengthen the climate and channels for upward communication, most organizations have formal or informal open-door policies. These systems allow employees to skip-jump supervisors—all the way to the CEO—if they feel they haven't had a fair hearing from lower-level supervisors.

But upward communication efforts represent the weakest link in the communication systems of typical American businesses, and in most companies, they are little more than window dressing. The value of open-door policies is quickly lost in the autocratic and bureaucratic workings of typical companies, along with fear of retribution from bypassed supervisors.

Anonymous upward communication systems are definitely more inviting to employees and, in many companies, serve as effective means of securing candid comments about company policies and actions. These programs require a high level of commitment and time on the part of management to provide prompt and honest answers to legitimate employee concerns. To be truly effective, these programs must operate as an adjunct to the chairman's office, with all the prestige and clout this relationship implies.

Some organizations have formal upward communication systems that work very effectively with this type of general arrangement: IBM's *Speak Up* is the best known and most emulated. Such programs allow employees to raise questions about company policies and actions—or about how they are treated on the job—and they permit them to do so with complete confidentiality. When operated successfully—with proper responses to every legitimate complaint or concern—these activities can have a very positive effect on employee attitudes and trust concerning management.

IBM Led the Way in Upward Communication

Although IBM's *Speak Up* program was considered a revolutionary concept when first established in 1959, it has since become a cornerstone of the company's employee communication process, having received more than 300,000 letters from employees and retirees over the years. (For more information on *Speak Up*, see Case Example 2 on IBM's employee communication system at the end of this chapter, pages 37-40.)

United Technologies Corporation (UTC) has a *Dialog* program modeled along the lines of *Speak Up*. But primary responsibility for administering the activity rests with UTC's business units, with guidance and consultative support from corporate staff. United Technologies has an unusual second tier in its upward communication system, a corporate ombudsman who also directs the *Dialog* activity.

Bob Morrissey of UTC says of his ombudsman post:

> This position has proven very effective as a direct two-way communication channel between UTC employees and senior management on virtually any subject of interest or concern to employees. It provides us with a cross-check of the most thorny employee problems or complaints, particularly those related to corporate policies and decisions.

The average number of queries which annually comes through *Dialog* runs to about 5,000, and more than 500 come through the ombudsman's office.

THREE-WAY COMMUNICATION

Emphasis on three-way communication is important. No division, plant, department or office is an island in the context of today's intensely competitive environment. Maximum effectiveness of any organization depends on a sharing of information, problems and improvements not only within the typical vertical structure of an organization, but also horizontally across the board.

The ideal communication system achieves maximum success working through the organizational structure—face-to-face, day-in and day-out. However, there are breakdowns in the official network in most organizations, which lead enlightened managers to install supplementary or "backup" channels—such as publications, bulletin boards and letters to employee homes.

An effective internal communication program obviously will contribute to an on-going sharing of information horizontally across an organization—as well as up and down. And certainly a strong effort to keep the entire management group up-to-date on latest developments is highly desirable. But starting at the very top, management people must assume a personal responsibility for instituting and encouraging information sharing both laterally at every level of the organization and as a normal part of managing.

THE SIX COMMANDMENTS OF EFFECTIVE COMMUNICATION

In the pursuit of a planned process of professional communication, there are six fundamental principles—basic commandments for the manager and the communicator.

1. Employee communication is a fundamental component of the organizational management system.

2. A clear statement of commitment by top management, as well as its participation and support, is essential.

3. Communication must be a planned process—there must be a strategy— involving both communication professionals and key management people.

4. Managers are the key conduits and catalysts for effective communication.

5. Priority business issues should be the core content of the employee communication program and should be discussed in an understandable and open manner through various channels of communication.

6. The communication system should undergo regular evaluation to prove its worth.

Let's look at each commandment in more detail.

COMMANDMENT NUMBER ONE:

Communication is a fundamental component of the management process and should be viewed as a contributing partner with other key staff functions in influencing employee understanding of both business goals and public relations issues.

Employee communication is a legitimate management discipline, one that can have a tremendous influence on the attitudes and work performance of employees. Employee communication programs, therefore, must be responsible for carrying their part of the management load, and they must be held accountable for the effectiveness of their activities. Their information priorities must be tied closely to the organization's business and public affairs goals.

Any professional who doesn't take a hard line on this point can't hope to sell the importance of the function, which is in competition with other activities for attention and support.

When dealing with tough-minded managers, speak their language. Because the communication activity needs to be sold constantly to management, cite its contributions or potential contributions both to organizational goals—and to the manager's own personal success.

Arbitrary censorship or personal prejudices should not be allowed to block the distribution of important facts—including previously sacred financial data—if this information can increase employee contributions without posing a "clear and present danger" to the company.

The same is true of background information on the corporation's stands on public issues. These are too often misunderstood or misstated by the public media, and they are transmitted, in all their negative flavor, to employees. It is no longer possible to have these matters handled by industry lobbyists in quiet sessions with lawmakers or their staffs. This is particularly true on such subjects as environmental and tax issues, where the company positions may, on the surface, often appear to be contrary to the best public interests.

On the other hand, if an employee communication program is expected to assume responsibilities in the same manner as other major staff disciplines, it must be called upon for counsel and advice by top management in matters affecting employee interests. It also should have the authority—and it should be expected—to make such recommendations on a regular basis. The communication function should have these responsibilities and this authority emphasized regularly by top management in policy statements, executive speeches, strategic plans and at management conferences.

The employee communication operation simply cannot get proper support throughout the management organization without being a very visible part of top management strategy and actions.

Another means of strengthening the basic foundation for employee communication as an integral part of the total business plan is to incorporate the major objectives of other key organizational functions—such as strategic planning, personnel, quality, marketing and labor relations—into the communication plan. This broadens both the content and the base of support for employee communication.

COMMANDMENT NUMBER TWO:

A clear statement of commitment by top managers is essential, as is their participation in and support of the communication process at all levels of the organization.

The establishment of an overall company policy on employee communication and of definitive guidelines for managers and supervisors is absolutely essential as a first step in securing broad management participation and support.

An official policy or mission statement establishes the philosophical, business and human-relations reasons for effective internal communication and should make clear how it differs from external communication. It articulates top management's commitment to open, honest communication as a way of life for the company, and it should clearly define basic principles and the practical, meaningful goals for effective communication systems.

Chevron Corporation, in its mission statement, says that "employees are the key to success—providing the fundamental vitality and reputation of our Company." The statement cites six objectives, one of which is:

> To foster a team spirit among all employees and involve them in the business objectives of the company...

We will provide a challenging and rewarding work environment, built on our commitment to open communication, teamwork, trust, personal development and recognition. Innovation, risk taking and an entrepreneurial approach are vital to our success.[1]

GM's policy statement, first issued in 1979, defines the basic principles behind company employee communication activities:

Effective two-way communications between management and employees is critical for success in our highly competitive worldwide business.

The need for employee understanding, involvement and cooperation has never been greater—and a broad base of information about the business is fundamental to the achievement of all these goals. More than ever, GM has an obligation to keep its employees informed about important matters that affect the business and their own livelihood.

Two-way information sharing can improve decision making and work performance by facilitating the making of decisions at the lowest possible levels by employees who know the most about getting the job done right. In turn, this increased participation can contribute to higher levels of employee satisfaction and quality of work life. We need ideas and suggestions from all employees about how to operate more effectively—at every level of the business. Good communications also can promote better employee understanding and consequent support for the corporation's positions on key public issues.[2]

Guidelines for Management

"Guidelines for Management" should be a companion document that provides specific guidance on principles of communication, recommended minimum standards and examples of the types of corporate and local information which should be spotlighted in employee communication programs. This is particularly important for multi-location organizations. Guidelines for management in a typical multi-location company should recommend the appointment of a coordinator at each location who will develop and manage the system. They also should define minimum standards against which performance evaluations of organizations can be made. The com-

[1]The employee publication of Chevron Corporation, *Chevron Focus* (August–September 1989), pp. 13–18.

[2]*Chairman's Letter on Employee Communications* signed by General Motors Chairman Roger B. Smith (October 12, 1983).

munication coordinator should be responsible for establishing a formal, organized program of regular communication with all employees, one involving key information about the business and its effect on employees. The following activities should be considered:

- Major emphasis on face-to-face communication that involves regular meetings between management and employees, including at least one state-of-the-business meeting per year with question-and-answer discussions.
- Regular, frequent publications for all employees.
- Periodic surveys to evaluate the effectiveness of employee communication activities and to provide direction for continuing improvements.

The guidelines should pay special attention to effective two-way communication within the supervisory structure. Sharing information among all managers should be encouraged, as well as upward communication of pertinent employee opinions, problems and ideas to higher levels of management.

Competition in Communication

Competition in American business and industry extends beyond products and certainly involves internal communication. Ford's top executives consider internal communication to be a strong competitive asset and guard many details of these activities as zealously as they do forward product secrets.

Ford's top-level endorsement of employee communication was stated forcefully by former Chairman Donald E. Petersen in his 1987 "Statement of Philosophy on Corporate Communications." This statement calls for "a deliberate openness in all of Ford's communication activities—with the news and information media and their customers, with the public at large, and with our own constituencies as well, both internal and external." It continues:

> Communication with our employees comes at the top of the list...One of our fundamental objectives is to establish trust with our employees. One avenue is by communicating with them honestly on the facts about the company, its actions and its points of view. This must include our problems and controversies, as well as our attributes and achievements...good news and bad.[3]

---

[3] Remarks delivered by Donald E. Petersen, former Chairman of the Ford Motor Co. to the Foundation for American Communications, Naples, Fla. (January 16, 1987).

Obviously, a piece of paper from corporate headquarters does not by itself produce good communication. It is also important that top management at each location make a strong commitment to its own managers and employees.

Management's role is not just passive support for the process and principles of good communication; it also involves participation on a day-to-day basis. Direct involvement and participation by management—at all levels—presents the strongest possible proof to employees that management's desire to communicate is for real.

COMMANDMENT NUMBER THREE:

Communication must be a planned process—a strategy—involving both communication professionals and key management people.

Development of a strategic plan, including short- and long-term goals, is necessary to put the employee communication function professionally on a par with other management disciplines. Ideally, the plan should be revised every year.

Its core should be the goals and objectives of the total organization, and key management people should be involved in its formulation. It is important that the strategic plan direct major attention to the issues which offer the greatest opportunities for the organization, as well as those which pose the most serious problems or potential dangers. The strategic plan also should take into consideration the major goals of related disciplines such as human resources, labor relations, management development and training. For organizations with unionized employees, special attention needs to be given to the regular distribution of information on the issues expected to be raised in contract negotiations. Input from employees should be sought in order that plans reflect not only management goals but also concerns and ideas of employees.

Continual reassessment of mission statements for the employee communication function forces regular self-analyses and updating of goals and objectives. Systematic distribution to and discussion of each year's plan among corporate and local communicators are essential.

To carry out its mission, the employee communication function must have full access to confidential information and plans at the highest levels, and regular, specific direction from top leaders.

This is critical if professionals are to develop effective communication plans which mesh with and complement strategies of other staff planners.

COMMANDMENT NUMBER FOUR:

Managers are the key conduits and catalysts for effective communication, and the system must recognize their need for information, training and rewards for good communication performance.

First and foremost, the top executives in any organization are responsible for establishing the policies, standards and environment for good communication. They also must perform as role models to show the rest of the management team that they practice what they preach.

Top managers should move around in their organization, visiting various parts of the operation and chatting with employees on a regular basis. Invisible managers build a wall of uncertainty, concern and disbelief between themselves and employees, so that the warm human aspects of management and communication are lost. Top executives should share important information with associates and subordinates and should encourage good communication within the organizations for which they are responsible. They need to be particularly sensitive to the upward flow of information and ideas—even if negative—and they need to ensure that deserving ideas or criticisms be acted upon or transmitted to the right persons for appropriate action.

Here's an example of support by personal involvement in a leadership role.

In late 1983, Bob Stempel (now GM's chairman but then general manager of Chevrolet) faced some tough decisions involving the permanent closing of a number of antiquated plants. One was the Flint Motor plant, employing about 1,000 people producing four- and six-cylinder engines, a plant with a history of serious labor problems dating back to the 1930s. When the decision had been made to close the plant permanently, the agony of who should tell the employees began. But Stempel said:

"As general manager, it's my ultimate decision to close the plant; I'll tell the employees." The plant had no conference area large enough to accommodate the entire work force. But Stempel wanted all of them to hear the news from him at the same time—before it

was announced to the press. So, in the plant cafeteria, they assembled representative employees from every department—totaling about 300 employees, supervisors and the entire UAW shop committee. And they installed closed-circuit television screens in several other plant rooms where the remainder of the employees could witness the meeting including a question-and-answer period.

The Lesson: The "top boss" does a better job than anyone else in handling a tough problem face-to-face and giving straight answers to employee questions and concerns.

Helping Managers Manage Better

One of the most critical assignments for communication specialists is to make sure that managers—from top to bottom—understand in the most basic way the tremendous potential of good communication in helping them manage people effectively. This is not a game people play, one which involves saying one thing and doing another, hiding fundamental facts from the employees who must do the work. It's a hard-nosed business principle. If you have your people on board in an informed, team-oriented way, you will get better team effort and results, along with happier employees.

Many professionals tend to view the chief executive officer as the main avenue to broad management support.

Certainly, that's important. But in most organizations of any size, that's the barest of beginnings if you want to develop a comprehensive, enduring system of employee communication, one which can become a fundamental part of the management structure and thinking.

As consultant Myron (Mike) Emanuel says:

> As communicators, we must constantly remind ourselves that we are not addressing a fixed audience of employees or CEOs, but a passing parade. The most logical approach, therefore, to continuing top management understanding and support is to direct your efforts not only to the chief executive officer but to the larger management group, among whom will be the future top executives.

Biggest Payoff at Local Levels

But beyond top-level support, every manager must accept his or her responsibility for two-way communication if the process is to produce the greatest benefits.

The truth is, a company's communication activities can only be as effective as their execution at local levels—and to a large degree by first-level supervisors. That's where credibility and relevance to employees are the highest.

Most surveys have shown that employees rank local management as the preferred source of information. The lower the organizational level of communication, the greater its relevance and credibility—and, therefore, its effectiveness. The immediate supervisor is first among various channels of local management communication—preferred and most trusted and also is far ahead of corporate management, the unions, the media and the grapevine, in that order.

Information from the local unit is considered the most important by employees because it relates to things about their own work group, plant, office or company. These are things that are more meaningful and have special relevance to their jobs and to their own job security.

Experience also shows that as local units improve their own communication processes, employees desire more corporate materials to fill in missing pieces of the information puzzle. A one-sided coin doesn't buy many groceries; neither does a one- sided communication effort. Only when the facts they receive from both company and local management sources become consistent, believable and relevant can employees put the "facts" they receive from the news media and grapevine into proper perspective.

But it is not enough to simply confer the mantle of responsibility for communication on managers and supervisors. It is essential to provide them with a regular flow of information from both corporate and local levels, training to make them more effective and confident communicators, and rewards for doing a good communication job.

COMMANDMENT NUMBER FIVE:

Priority business issues should be the core content of the employee communication program and should be discussed in an open and understandable manner through various channels of communication.

No communication should be undertaken that does not have a reason, that does not have a role in the overall strategic plan aimed at achieving organizational goals or satisfying legitimate employee information needs.

Employee communication activities should be governed by a mission statement understood by all members of the staff involved in the process and these activities should be supported by higher executives. Communicators need to be aggressive in showing management the potential of good communication and in showing how it can contribute to overall business goals—and also why management support is essential if a communication program is to achieve its full potential.

Content Extremely Important

Content is extremely important, as is the need to discuss both sides of controversial matters. Condensing company press releases won't do the job; employees will get this information from newspapers or on evening TV or radio newscasts. What employees really want is to have someone from management give them the reasons behind management announcements or events—maybe not today, but soon.

Too often, business executives seem to announce the solutions ("We're going to have layoffs") before they tell employees they all have a common problem ("Business is bad").

A steady flow of information about the business—its goals, problems and plans—can bring employees into a more participative, cooperative and satisfying relationship with management. And this information should be supplied on a continuing basis, which helps to establish durable credibility for the communication process and for management.

Focusing on the fact that employees are the primary customers of the communication activity helps to clarify desired activities and direction. This is true even if plans are sometimes overruled "in the interests of the total organization" or because of what the chief executive feels should be done. However, blind allegiance to higher executives in actions unfair to employees can have damaging effects on management-employee relations.

Principles of Good Communication

Defining content is a big first step. But there are a number of other critical elements which will determine how successfully an organization's messages are transmitted to employees and whether they are believed.

In a discussion of basic principles of good communication in *Effective Public Relations,* authors Scott Cutlip, Allen Center and Glen Broom give special emphasis to the elements of content, context, continuity, consistency and credibility:

- *Content.* The message must have meaning for the receiver and be compatible with the person's values and needs.
- *Context.* A communication program must square with the realities of its environment and must provide for participation and playback. Mechanical media are only supplementary to the words and deeds of daily living—i.e. to face-to-face communication.
- *Continuity and consistency.* Communication is an unending process which requires repetition in various forms, and its messages must be consistent.
- *Credibility.* Communication starts with a climate of belief and confidence built by the performance of the institution over time.[4]

Advice from Dr. Seuss. Theodor Seuss Geisel—better known as Dr. Seuss, the author of children's books—offered some sage advice to a graduating class at Lake Forest College in Illinois in one of the shortest commencement addresses on record. Its message applies equally well to communication professionals aiming for high credibility in their efforts:

My uncle ordered popovers
from the restaurant's bill of fare.
And, when they were served,
he regarded them with a penetrating stare.
Then he spoke great Words of Wisdom
as he sat there on that chair:
"To eat those things," said my uncle,
"You must exercise great care.
You may swallow down what's solid...
But you must spit out the air!"

[4] Scott M.Cutlip, Allen H.Center and Glen M.Broom, *Effective Public Relations* (Englewood Cliffs, N.J.: Prentice-Hall, 1985), pp. 283–84.

Dr. Seuss concluded,

And…as you partake of the world's bill of fare,
that's darned good advice to follow.
Do a lot of spitting out the hot air.
And be careful what you swallow.

Too much hot air, like half-truths or no truths, can wreak havoc with credibility.

Credibility Is Critical

Without credibility, communication activities are largely wasted effort and money. Credibility is a precious part of an institution's character which is reflected to employees. It results from countless impressions involving the relationship between employer and employee, between supervisor and worker, and among all members of the company team.

All communication messages, received through both internal and external channels, contribute to how employees rate the believability of management. Equally important, the characteristic of credibility can be adversely affected by what management doesn't say or says in a muddy or devious way.

Eastern Airlines Example. Scott Cutlip places special importance on credibility and context.

Unless an audience has confidence and respect in the communication source, the message is likely to be shrugged aside as unbelievable or irrelevant. But credibility alone is not sufficient. Because messages are interpreted in the context, or environment, in which they are received, a climate of belief is essential for truly effective communication.

A prime illustration of these fundamentals can be found in the Eastern Airlines strike in 1989. Frank Lorenzo, president of the parent Texas Air Corporation, found that Eastern employees did not believe him, or the messages received in the context of a strike, nor did they believe fears he projected that Eastern would never fly again. Lorenzo's Texas-booted tactics brought a new strength and solidarity to organized labor not often seen in recent years.

Nissan Philosophy. A similar example, this one favoring management, came in the summer of 1989 in a bid by the United Auto Workers to represent employees at the Smyrna, Tennessee, assembly plant of the Nissan Motor Manufacturing Corporation.

The vote was what *The Wall Street Journal* called "a humiliating" 2–1 defeat for the UAW, and it came after a hard-fought, 18-month campaign by both sides.

The union blamed the loss on a "sustained anti-union campaign" that created a "climate of fear" within the plant. It also charged excessive work place demands and gross health and safety standards.

Nissan officials, however, said the union failed to give the workers a substantive reason to support a union. They pointed out that wages and benefits of Nissan workers were comparable to the levels in plants with workers organized by the UAW and that no layoffs had occurred at the Smyrna assembly plant since it opened six years earlier.

The New York Times said, "Nissan has spent a great deal of time and effort educating technicians and involving them in decisions on everything from new vehicle models to market penetration and profit margins."

The Chattanooga Times said, "The company's strategy is based on the philosophy that loyal and contented employees will build better automobiles more economically than workers who feel they are adversaries of management." The newspaper also said that workers say that the company "pays well and treats them fairly. But equally important is the fact that the company encourages them to use their intelligence and imagination to make the plant run better."

Again, there was obviously "a climate of belief" fostered by Nissan management, one which was built over time and could not be blown away in the crisis climate of a union representation battle.

Union Carbide Tragedy. The company faced one of the worst industrial disasters in history in December 1984 when leaking gas at the Bhopal, India plant killed 3,000 people and critically injured thousands more. At the first summit meeting of UCC executives and corporate communication officials, five priority communication goals were approved. As Bob Berzok, UCC's corporate communications director, said:

Credibility was at the top of the list—first and foremost. We agreed that, regardless of the merits of the company's position or the facts in the case, nothing would be achieved without a high level of credibility in every aspect of reporting—to both internal and external audiences. Our total communication plan was predicated on that fundamental goal."

(Union Carbide's five-year Bhopal communication program is discussed in Case Example 3 at the end of this chapter, pages 41-44.)

Other Media Supplement Face-to-Face Communication

It's been said repeatedly that face-to-face discussions are the most effective form of communication. It is the most preferred and believed—one which provides the opportunity for two-way exchanges, immediate responses and the greatest warmth and personal feeling.

But print and visual media also should be used on a regular basis—as a supplement to face-to-face information sharing or to fill the gap when the person-to-person network falls down. Under most conditions, in fact, the print media is considered the most fundamental source for quick, consistent, dependable communication.

Electronic newslines provide a rapid, inexpensive medium for transmitting important company news, which can then be distributed to key managers, posted on bulletin boards and reprinted in local newsletters. An effective corporate-wide system of employee publications can serve as a valuable network for communicating priority information about both corporate and local business activities.

Corporate videotape and film messages can carry quite an impact, particularly if combined with local presentations or used by first-level supervisors as discussion starters. Satellite TV can be particularly effective for management communication in multi-plant companies, and down the road it offers great potential for regular interactive communication sessions between corporate and field management.

The secret to any successful employee communication program is to make use of essentially all media in a coordinated effort, one which articulates key messages, states them in a variety of ways to capture everyone's attention and repeats them over time to reinforce their importance to the people and the organization.

COMMANDMENT NUMBER SIX:

The communication process should undergo regular evaluation to prove its worth in terms of employee-management relations as well as employee performance and awareness of key public issues.

It is essential that the communication function be tested periodically to determine its effectiveness and to give directions for improvements.

How do you measure whether you're getting your messages across to employees, or whether employees understand and go along with management plans and actions? Do they believe what management says? What evidence do you have to show management that your function is carrying its share of the load and is worth what it's spending?

Lack of Research Tools

The inability to answer these questions with hard, scientific data is one of the major handicaps to full recognition of the employee communication function. In these highly competitive times, value received for dollars invested is a rule which is—and should be—applied to every activity.

The relationship of communication to bottom-line results is at best still fuzzy, although recent and current research activities project optimism. More public and private organizations are being forced by pressures of competition and tight money to evaluate both traditional and new activities to see if they are working effectively—and, if not, what improvements should be made.

Progress in communication research may come in terms of helping the organization make more money—for example, by the increased involvement of employees in continuing improvement activities. But it also may come as ways are developed to measure the effectiveness of communication efforts that save the organization money—such as providing better background information to employees on negotiation issues or building opposition to unfair government regulations.

Researching employee and management opinions about communication effectiveness can be done informally by in-house professionals in a variety of ways. Talking to employees, individually and in groups, can give you candid and often gutsy comments about how well you're doing. Telephone or publication readership surveys can also provide useful information. Focus-group discussions on the total program and also on major segments should be a regular procedure in top-notch employee communication systems. But informal surveys and in-house studies are subject to credibility questions by discerning managers—and that's understandable. Outside consultants can provide solid, credible evaluations through what is called a comprehensive audit—which management usually will perceive as a more objective evaluation process. The comprehensive audit can be a valuable measurement of employee and management perceptions of current communication effectiveness, and it can provide direction for future improvements.

The important thing is to get the communication system on a regular evaluation-and-redirection cycle—whether it's done in-house or by outside consultants. It's essential for a strong program and management support.

SUMMARY

It is important to view the internal communication function as a fundamental process of a modern management organization prepared to be judged in terms of sound planning, contribution to organizational goals and service value to other key functions of management.

The communication activity should operate with both short- and long-term strategic plans which are based on overall company plans. Its success depends heavily on management support, not only in helping to develop overall goals and information priorities but also in executing the communication process at every level of the organization.

The communication professional must be aggressive in developing creative approaches, in using the latest technology and techniques, in involving managers at all levels and in establishing a regular system for evaluating the effectiveness of the communication process.

The "six commandments" constitute key elements for a modern employee communication system performing as a full-fledged member of the management team, one capable of paying its own way and of favorably influencing bottom-line results and employee morale.

CASE 2

International Business Machines Corporation

STRONG TWO-WAY
EMPLOYEE
COMMUNICATION SYSTEM

International Business Machines (IBM) wrote the book on upward communication thirty years ago with the introduction of its *Speak Up* program, and still considers it one of the most important aspects of an extensive employee communication system. But IBM also uses many other channels of personal, print and visual media, with increasing emphasis on satellite television and videotapes.

Like many other major U.S. companies, IBM in the late 1980s underwent extensive changes designed to meet unprecedented global competition—through improved quality, efficiency and response to customer needs. Included were the restructuring of worldwide business operations into seven major business units, the introduction of expanded product offerings which were to be brought to market quicker, the flattening of its organizational structure and the closing of five U.S. manufacturing plants. IBM also trimmed its U.S. work force from nearly 243,000 in 1985 to 206,000 in 1990.

"In this dramatically changing business environment, employee communication has become much more critical," says Les Simon, vice president of communications for IBM United States.

All of these changes, if not explained properly, can dramatically erode employee confidence and loyalty. It is important that employees understand what is going on, the reasons for all these changes, what they mean to the company and what they mean to them as employees.

This is particularly true in a technical company like IBM where things are moving fast, you have a highly-educated work force and very intense competition. In times like these, employees want to know how they can help. So, we try to provide them with information for better understanding our business, motivating them to be better performers on their jobs and creating other avenues for contributions through suggestions and criticism. That's why we place special emphasis on a two-way exchange of ideas and information, including IBM's *Speak Up,* Suggestion Program and "Open Door" policy.

PUBLICATIONS PLAY IMPORTANT ROLE

IBM's lineup of employee publications is impressive.

Think is a high-quality, four-color magazine mailed bi-monthly to all 200,000 employees at home. It usually runs twenty-four to forty-eight pages in length and covers a wide variety of subjects about IBM operations, management philosophy and people around the world. Heavy emphasis is on the "market-driven" aspects—products, customers, customer services, how to be a market-driven employee and why.

The market-driven emphasis is even stronger in the bi-monthly publications for IBM's major units—seven business organizations, U.S. Marketing and Services Division and Research Division.

IBM also publishes a quarterly *Management Report* for its 7,000 managers around the world. It is two-color, and runs twenty to twenty-four pages in tabloid format. The publication provides in-depth coverage of major company decisions, developments, plans and problems, with special emphasis on serving the customer. The report is designed to keep managers up to date on IBM and industry developments and to help them communicate better with employees.

OTHER CORPORATE RESPONSIBILITIES

The internal communication staff also is responsible for:

- Producing videotapes for the corporation and for major units, involving about fifty a year, directed both at management and employee audiences. These videotapes are heavily oriented toward business news and personnel information and services.

- Developing a satellite network that will ultimately involve up to 800 U.S. locations plus overseas sites. Informational programs for both employees and management will be a part of the regular menu for IBM's television network.

- Developing annual IBM internal communication plans which are shared with all major units on an advisory basis.

- Operating a computer information system which gives local communicators and virtually all IBM employees their own electronic bulletin boards—updated constantly through their personal computers. Each of IBM's manufacturing and development sites in North America has its own local publications.

- Directing several regional one-day training and business update conferences for communicators each year.

Simon says that annual employee surveys give IBM's internal communication activities high marks. Chief criticisms, directed mainly at publications, are about timeliness and candor. He believes increasing use of television will allow IBM to be more responsive in both of these areas.

SPEAK UP A 30-YEAR SUCCESS STORY

IBM's Speak Up program, in 30 years of operation, received more than 300,000 letters from employees and retirees located in sixty countries.

The program encourages employees to criticize any work-related situation and to get straightforward answers promptly from top-level IBM executives. Critical to its long-term success has been top management's absolute guarantee of anonymity and protection against any form of retribution. Identity of employees are known only to the local Speak Up administrator.

Employees signing their names receive a personal letter at their home addresses—an answer from the appropriate IBM executives—usually within ten working days. Or if they wish, their Speak Up administrator will arrange a private phone call or interview to discuss the subject of concern. Simon says:

> Our Speak Up program provides a confidential means of resolving or at least explaining prickly problems or serious concerns of employees. But it also is a productive avenue for employee ideas and gives management a continual reading of employee thinking and needs, particularly in areas relating to their jobs and the work environment.

Virtually anything on employees' minds is grist for the mill, says Mike Zimet, who directs the worldwide Speak Up program.

> The program responds to questions in hundreds of categories, including office equipment, security, cost effectiveness, employee-manager relations, environment, safety and a wide variety of company policies. We even get a few kudos from time to time.

Some critics say upward communication programs such as *Speak Up* undermine the basic relationship between managers and their people. In fact, this has been a major reason why the concept has not been successful in many companies. Not true at IBM, Simon says, where surveys indicate that managers regard the program as a valuable alternative communication channel for employees.

Simon believes the employee communication function will have an increasingly important role in the 1990s. He feels this assignment will be more difficult because of the growing complexity of the work place and increasing employee demands for more quality information. He believes satellite TV will enhance IBM's capabilities for credible two-way communication with both employees and managers.

```
CASE 3
Union Carbide Corporation
```

LESSONS IN CRISIS COMMUNICATION
FROM
BHOPAL TRAGEDY

Union Carbide Corporation (UCC) faced a communication crisis of mammoth proportions in December 1984 when leaking gas at the Bhopal, India, plant left more than 3,000 people dead and thousands more critically injured.

Special communication efforts were required through 1989, when the company agreed to pay the $470 million in damages ordered by the Indian Supreme Court. A five-year crisis of that magnitude should be enough to qualify Bob Berzok, Union Carbide's corporate communication director, as a leading advocate of comprehensive crisis plans.

But he isn't!

GOOD DAY-TO-DAY COMMUNICATION BEST

As a matter of fact, Berzok believes that a crisis communication plan is only needed if your company doesn't have an effective on-going communication system, one that operates in good times and bad. He said that in the Bhopal incident, UCC didn't change the way it communicated.

It just used an established, respected system to communicate that much more information to meet greatly expanded demands.

Too many companies devote enormous amounts of time, money and staff effort in developing massive crisis communication plans instead of taking that same time, money and effort to shore up their existing, day-to-day communication systems. This would provide them with not only a more effective year-round communication activity but one that could handle emergency situations very well and with a high level of credibility established over time.

The Bhopal communication task was complicated for a number of reasons. The plant was in a remote location, with only two international telephone lines in the area. There were language barriers and lawsuit settlement prospects were deeply mired in Indian politics. Expectations for compensation were beyond reality. Also, there was an almost unbelievable demand for company statements by both the external media and employees.

But the company's crises didn't end with Bhopal. During the traumatic 1985–89 period, a series of other major crises wracked Union Carbide. Included were the immediate drop in the price of company stock from $55 to $32 a share; an attempted hostile takeover by GAF Corporation; a gas leak at the company's Institute, West Virginia, plant; an extensive reorganization of the Union Carbide business; major divestitures involving assets of more than $700 million; and financial recapitalizations.

MAJOR ROLE FOR TOP EXECUTIVES

When disaster struck in December 1984, Union Carbide public affairs staff members and top corporate executives—including Chairman Warren Anderson and President Alec Flamm—sat down and mapped out a broad strategy. Three major communication decisions were made immediately:

- The existing communication system would be used as much as possible for both internal and external audiences.
- Press conferences would be held as often as warranted as a result of new information that could be corroborated. Daily news briefings were held for the first 3 weeks.
- Distribution of new information would be made as broadly as possible to both internal and external audiences worldwide at the same time.

Berzok says:

Prior to Bhopal, Union Carbide was not on the leading edge of communication, but was basically a low-profile operation. Fortunately, redirection of corporate communication efforts in the early 1980s gave increased attention to the employee audience and the press media as well. So, we were better prepared for Bhopal.

The increased communication demands were dramatic. In the year following Bhopal, press requests increased from an average of 250 a year to more than 5,000; employee bulletins increased from annual levels of forty-to-fifty to more than 200; and employee videotapes increased from three-to-five a year to forty-five. In 1988, ten videotapes and 200 employee bulletins were distributed.

Videotapes of press conferences on Bhopal were distributed the same day for worldwide overnight delivery to broadcast stations in major Carbide-plant communities. Tapes were shipped unedited for maximum credibility.

Chairman Warren Anderson was an active participant in Union Carbide's communication program, stating the company's position through speeches to plants and plant-community groups and also regularly through the use of employee videotapes.

GOALS OF COMMUNICATION PLAN

The UCC communication effort had five major goals:

1. *Credibility.* This was *the* goal, first and foremost. Regardless of the merits of the company's position or the facts of the case, nothing would be achieved without a high level of credibility in every aspect of reporting.
2. *Timeliness.* It was vital to get Union Carbide's side of the story out as quickly and completely as possible to reduce potential rumors or false information.
3. *Range.* The company would be extending the geographic boundaries of UCC's communication sphere from one that was traditionally domestic to a truly international information network.
4. *Viability.* The company needed to demonstrate to employees that Union Carbide represented a basically sound, viable enterprise which would go on with its normal business. Employee performance and confidence in the company should not be diminished.
5. *Accuracy.* The company needed to get across to the public and employees the fact that solid evidence (uncovered during a 2-year investigation) indicated the Bhopal tragedy was the result of employee sabotage—and it had to make this point without backing off from the company's "moral responsibility" for the disaster.

The basic strength of Union Carbide as a worldwide industrial enterprise was demonstrated dramatically as a result of the defeat of GAF's hostile takeover attempt—and even after spending $58 million for the Bhopal litigation, the company posted 1988 record earnings per share.

Berzok is proud of the United Carbide corporate communications staff and expresses confidence in its ability to handle almost any kind of crisis. In fact, he says that during the 5-year period, "Our people went through experiences equalling what might be expected in a normal 50-year career in the communication field."

MAKE THE MOST OF CRISES

Berzok says that companies that do experience a crisis should make the most of it—once it's over. This can be done either by impressing on top management the need for strengthening existing communication activities or by emphasizing how much better the emergency could have been handled if an established, credible system had been in place. "Bhopal taught us two other fundamental lessons," Berzok says:

> The first was that we should "Never say never" or "It can't happen here" when it comes to predicting what might happen, particularly in safety-related areas. It may be true, but people find it hard to believe—and therefore tend to suspect your credibility in general.
>
> The second lesson is that communication—including media relations, employee communication and investor communication—is much more effective during emergencies as a corporate function rather than being decentralized to operating units.

Bhopal resulted in substantial improvements in the company's total communication program, he pointed out.

> Union Carbide communicates much more effectively on a day-to-day basis, with increased credibility and much stronger emphasis on international operations than we did before 1985. We have been able to institute some important fundamental improvements such as communication training for plant managers, media training for our executives and some new community relations activities.
>
> Perhaps most important is the increased recognition and respect which the communication function now enjoys from management at all levels—not only for its demonstrated professionalism but also the fundamental importance of communication as a part of the management process.

Chapter 3

The Communication Process: Building the System and Structure to Last

Veteran professionals will tell you that employee communication advances can be very transitory. They arrive trumpeted as miracle solutions to our problems but often fade away almost before the eye of the storm has passed.

To reach its ultimate potential, the employee communication function must earn its place at the management table. And it must be done so convincingly that it becomes an accepted part of the woodwork, something that the organization simply can't do without if it wants to be successful. It must become an integral part of the management structure, making valuable, continuing contributions over the long haul.

To accomplish this task, the employee communication system must be organized in a productive, efficient, imaginative manner that brings recognition and respect from the most critical executives as well as acceptance by the prime audience—employees. Good performance adds to its stature and the magnitude of its responsibilities.

MANY SYSTEMS OPERATE ON HIT-OR-MISS BASIS

However, many internal communication functions aren't organized in a business-like fashion. They operate on a hit-or-miss basis, without established mission, planned goals and evaluation processes. They concentrate too heavily on employee publications, neglecting other media in building an effective total system. Too many of their efforts are reactive or defensive in nature; they do not display the long-range perspective and purpose which gives professional stature and performance to the process.

The previous chapter discussed six key elements in an effective employee communication system. This chapter will build on these pillars of strength, adding elements which give further vitality and texture to what can be a productive management resource. Included will be the importance of strategic planning, closer ties between line managers and communicators, proactive versus reactive communication, the importance of corporate services to local units and the responsibilities of the communication manager.

Employee communication efforts have graduated from the horse-and-buggy era. Those were the days featuring little more than house organs, bulletin board notices and, when the company was in trouble, letters to employee homes or frantic news conferences with spinoff releases for employees.

In the past, traditional employee communication programs placed major emphasis on activities designed to reach the total employee group. But since the early 1980s, some companies have been giving increasing attention to communicating with their management groups and to strengthening the role of managers in the employee communication system.

PROACTIVE AND MANAGER-ORIENTED SYSTEMS

The more progressive employee communication systems are proactive, planned processes, rather than reactive, firefighting mechanisms. They are guided by company policy and guidelines which place a high priority on internal communication, with specific responsibilities being delegated to each and every manager. And they use a diversified media attack of specially-tailored informational materials for employees and for managers.

A significant change is also occurring in the way companies assign accountability for employee communication, with major responsibility being pushed down to line management. In turn, the role of the professional communicator is being reoriented toward providing more support services to help managers communicate better.

It is a changing pattern that will ally professional communicators much more closely with managers of people in seeking to accelerate the process of change and the acceptance of the new leadership culture.

Communicators must become facilitators in helping managers manage better through effective communication.

Roger D'Aprix, of the management consulting firm of William M. Mercer, Inc., says:

> Some communicators make the dangerous assumption that managers can't handle the demanding communication job these days, and that only we as professionals really know how to carry it off.
>
> So, we skip along, pretending we're indispensable. In the meantime, we fail to look for ways to equip managers, develop a communication strategy that can be handled as part of their normal leadership responsibilities, and with us serving as backup.
>
> We must become experts in helping to facilitate the people-management process. That clearly means we have to step out of the simple role of producers of publications and "programs" and become broad process facilitators. This may be a painful transition for many of us. But in the best of all worlds, that's what we ought to become—backups or facilitators—in helping managers manage better through effective communication.

CLOSER BONDS BETWEEN COMMUNICATORS AND MANAGERS

This trend toward closer working relationships between managers and communicators will strengthen the role of employee communication in the years ahead, according to Jack McNulty, former vice president of public relations for General Motors.

McNulty says there are strong pressures in GM for improved communication and trust between management and employees, but that another generation of managers will probably have to be phased out before the concept of open communication is fully accepted.

> In General Motors today, there is a remarkable degree of candor and self-criticism in our internal publications and videotapes that would have been impossible even five years ago.

There will always be some proprietary information that should not be communicated to the public, even our own employees...Management, of course, must represent the interests of both employees and shareholders. We have to be sure we're getting the most productivity for our compensation dollar. And we must do this in ways that don't shortchange our employees and yet will enhance their jobs with more involvement and a greater sense of fulfillment.

McNulty believes the most important exercise in communication is on the plant floor—"supervisor to employee, one to one." To bring significant improvement in communication at that level, he says, will require a change in corporate attitude and a reorientation of supervisor responsibilities to make information sharing a top priority *in fact.*

In the future, line managers will have a much more important role in the information-sharing process, particularly the first-level supervisor. No supervisor can manage effectively today without being a good communicator—and this will be even more so in the future.

Corporate management will become more facilitators than doers in helping local units and their managers do the major share of the communication job. That's where it really belongs. Corporate communication functions will provide encouragement, effective information-sharing and audit systems and whatever other services are necessary to facilitate good communication by managers at every company location.

KEY RESOURCE OF LINE MANAGEMENT

Ray O'Connell, division manager of public relations for AT&T, also believes that employee communication is a primary responsibility of line management. He says, "The work done by a functional group such as employee communication staffs charged with the formal communication job (such as print and visuals) must support line managers in fulfilling this responsibility."

He cites four actions needed to carry out this goal:

- Clearly identify communication responsibilities and expectations of both the communicator and the line manager.
- Build into all manager training programs a core segment on manager communication, skills and potentials.
- Support managers at all levels with timely and credible formal vehicles of information sharing.

- As part of overall evaluation of communication activities, measure how much they help managers to be better communicators.

"The key," O'Connell says, "is to make sure that the information carried by the formal communication vehicles is in sync with the realities of the work place."

If it doesn't serve a useful need in the trenches of the business, the communication function has failed in one of its most fundamental roles. And it will be shrugged off as irrelevant—or worse, it will be resented by managers as wasteful aggravation.

STRATEGIC PLANNING

Broad-based strategic planning is essential. Its core should be the business goals of the organization—with special emphasis on the efforts to incorporate key public relations and human resources objectives as much as possible. The employee communication director has the responsibility of developing both short- and long-range plans for his or her operation. These should be submitted to higher levels of management on an annual basis for their information or review and comments.

Dr. James E. Grunig, co-author and editor of a progress report on a major research project for the International Association of Business Communicators, says that "excellent organizations practice communication strategically"—i.e., with a long-term perspective, not on a hit-and-miss basis with major emphasis on short-term results. Excellent organizations, Grunig continues, "develop programs to communicate with publics, both external and internal, that provide the greatest threats to, and opportunities for, the organization."[1]

Five Steps for Effective Strategic Plan

Grunig, a professor at the University of Maryland College of Journalism, says that strategic public relations—internal or external—are divided into five steps. He emphasizes the need to

[1] James E. Grunig, ed., *Excellence in Public Relations and Communication Management: Contributions to Effective Organizations,*, (Hillsdale, N.J.: Lawrence Erlbaum Associates, forthcoming, 1991).

direct special efforts toward important segments of an organization's total audience.

Here are the five steps he feels are necessary in developing and carrying out an effective strategic plan:

1. *Identify issues important to the organization and then manage the organization's response.* This is normally referred to as "issues management," and the basic principles should apply to both external and internal communication activities, although priority rankings and emphasis of audience messages may vary, too. Efficiency, quality, employee benefits, competition and government affairs are examples of high-interest internal issues. If possible, rank them in order of priority to ensure proper emphasis to each.

2. *Segment the publics that respond differently to those issues.* Management, employees, stockholders and retirees are obvious segments of the so-called family audience. Many companies also target union leadership, financial analysts or suppliers for special communication.

3. *Identify objectives for communication programs.* Specifically, what is the program designed to achieve—immediately and in a year or more—in support of overall organizational goals? Top management input can make these objectives more relevant and more acceptable to management.

4. *Plan communication programs based on these organizational objectives.* Selection of media, degree of emphasis and frequency, and coordination with other communication activities of the organization are basic to producing a coordinated total communication effort.

5. *Evaluate the effects of communication activities in helping to achieve organizational objectives.* Use of both formal and informal research methods on all major activities is desirable.

Lack of Direction and Information

One of the biggest problems faced by many employee communication managers is lack of direction and substantive information from the highest levels of their companies. In most cases, this function still operates several levels removed from the CEO, and too much of the direction comes from crisis or panic situations.

As Roger D'Aprix says:

> The crucial step that is so often omitted is for management and the communication professionals to agree on organizational issues themselves...The failure to identify and articulate the vital issues of the organization dooms the communication effort to a formless and confusing message that generally makes reactive communication the only workable method of operation.[2]

Employee Role in Strategic Planning

Bob Davis, retired president of Chevron Chemical, likes to describe a dramatic change in his own perceptions about employee communication—from a "need-to-know" philosophy to one which reached out to involve the entire Chevron work force in the company's strategic planning process.

Davis says, "People will respond heartily if you involve them in the business planning process and share the information that comes out of it. Everyone wants to be part of a team, and we ought to let them."[3]

Don't Underestimate Employee Intelligence

Some of my associates talk about the fear of information overload. Generally speaking, however, people today are pretty sophisticated and have a tremendous appetite and capacity for information about what's happening. This is particularly true if the news affects them, their livelihood and their family's financial security.

Allan Csiky, GM's director of employee communications, agrees:

> I think—and our research confirms this—that the average employee is smarter than anyone seems to think he or she is. As a result, too often we underestimate the intelligence of our employees to assimilate and understand the truth, difficult and negative though it may

[2]From Roger D'Aprix, *Communicating for Productivity* (New York: Harper & Row, Publishers, Inc., 1982), p. 87. Copyright © 1982 by Roger D'Aprix. Reprinted by permission of Harper & Row, Publishers, Inc.

[3]The employee publication of Chevron Corporation, *Chevron Focus* (August–September 1989), pp. 13–14.

be. Although telling employees bad news may create short-term
morale problems with some, over the long term, being honest with
people makes them full partners in the enterprise. They feel freer to
offer their ideas.

As Sandy MacKie, employee communication manager for
Chevron, says, "Management gets considerable advice about the
dangers of saying too much or being too explicit. They need others
to counsel them on the risks of communicating too little."

If there is a choice, communicators should err on the side of too
much information—not too little. Employees are smart enough to
sort out what they want and need—and to blow away the chaff.

In a well-coordinated internal/external public relations plan,
the internal communication media should be a primary outlet for
good stories about the company.

It's an opportunity to get broader exposure for in-depth, more
human interest stories than are normally handled by news-rela-
tions people. If these stories contribute to a better understanding
of management actions among employees, they should have a similar beneficial effect on external audiences.

"Information Priorities"

The regular development of "information priorities"—in con-
cert with top executives—provides a valuable strategic tool in coordinating substantive information for both corporate and local
activities.

Management conferences represent an ideal base from which
to construct or update information priorities geared to the most
important problems, plans and business goals of the organization.
If such meetings are held annually, they provide an ideal, high-level
and timely source for keeping employee communication activities
right on target.

Annual information priorities force the internal communication manager to establish the most important subjects and issues
on a regular basis and to translate them into specific priorities to
guide both corporate and local communication efforts. They also can
be useful for advanced news coverage on problem subjects for
important upcoming events, such as annual stockholder meetings
and labor negotiations.

Labor Negotiations Need a Special Plan

Labor contract negotiations should be part of the year-in and year-out strategic plan for employee communication—with special attention being given to the subject during the year or so preceding actual union-management discussions.

The most effective communication plan for labor negotiations is that which does not have the appearance of a campaign or of corporate propaganda. The year-round practice of substantive communication of important information about the business is basic. If new and supplemental information is inserted into an on-going system of communication, it will generally be viewed with a much higher degree of credibility.

Costs of health care, absenteeism and poor product quality are the kinds of subjects which should be discussed on a regular basis, but intensified in the year or so prior to contract negotiations.

COMMUNICATION SYSTEMS CAN BE MANAGED

In advancing the role of managers in the day-to-day process of information sharing, it is important to persuade them that the communication process can be managed—consciously and methodically—in ways that support their organizational and personal objectives. That's not to say that the flow of all business information can be controlled—or even that this goal is desirable in today's "full-disclosure" environment.

But a core of regular business information can be channeled systematically and efficiently through the entire management organization.

This will provide a consistent, credible foundation of knowledge to counter rumors and misinformation and give employees solid direction. It will also help to establish stability and respect in the communication process itself among both managers and employees.

COMMUNICATION IN MANY ORGANIZATIONS IS REACTIVE

Ron Actis, director of public affairs for GM's automotive components group, believes that a planned, systematic flow of business information through the management organization is the essential core for any effective communication system. Once this foundation is established, print and visual media can strengthen and reinforce the face-to-face information sharing between managers and employees. (Saginaw Division's employee communication system is discussed in Case Example 4 at the end of this chapter on pages 64-67.)

Unfortunately, the pattern of communication in many organizations is not planned, but reactive. News of the event flows almost immediately through informal channels, popularly called the grapevine, or is picked up by a news reporter from the grapevine and is broadcast by mass media.

Most of the time, official news releases on major news affecting employees will be slower than the grapevine. Even professionals marvel at how quickly the information flows through an organization via the grapevine—and the more negative the news, the faster it moves and the more distorted it becomes.

Communicating through formal channels—such as news releases, employee meetings or the distribution of other printed or visual materials—can provide a strong element of accuracy and authority which helps employees interpret events properly. But management releases are too often so sanitized or so filled with legalese or personnelese that important facts are obscured or even excluded. The result is communication confusion or chaos—and this results in big shell holes in management's credibility.

But with or without communication from management, employees will find out what happened and will filter and interpret what it means to them and to their organization. They will speculate on the causes and motives of management, and they will add their own perceptions and beliefs. The fewer facts they have from official sources, the bigger the chances for speculation and negative conclusions.

REACTIVE VERSUS PROACTIVE COMMUNICATION

Roger D'Aprix, in his book *Communicating for Productivity,* has an extensive discussion of the advantages of the proactive versus the reactive process of communication. He believes that organizational communicators have a basic responsibility to develop proactive communication systems which allow them to manage the system rather than having events run the process.[4]

[4] From Roger D'Aprix, *Communicating for Productivity* (New York: Harper & Row, Publishers, Inc., 1982, pp. 42-57)

Clearly, the reactive process has serious limitations. By focusing on what happened, not "why" or "what" it means, it forces employees to speculate on the reasons for and the expected effects of management actions. And it forces them to do so amid waves of rumors, false information and very often, anti-management opinions from the unions, news media or disgruntled employees. The inability of management to be the prime source of prompt information also weakens its credibility.

In contrast, the proactive system, practiced on a continuing basis, offers several important advantages for both managers and communicators:

- It gives management the opportunity to discuss issues, priorities and action plans—providing a broad base of understanding about the business, one not tied to big-ticket or emergency events.

- It allows management to convey information in an orderly and planned manner—in many cases preparing employees for tough decisions down the road.

- It helps to ensure that the impact of the event is as clear and positive as possible to employees—including reasons for management decisions and their probable impact on employees.

- It promotes employee understanding, trust and confidence in management.

- Carried on over time, the proactive process will build a solid base of credibility for management and its communication efforts.

As D'Aprix points out, the proactive system has definite advantages, not only for professional communicators but for managers as well. In the book *Inside Organizational Communication,* he says:

With a proactive system, communication becomes a manageable process rather than an afterthought or an attempt to explain what went wrong or to defend why something was done. The reactions of various constituencies are anticipated and addressed as the policy or program is being implemented. In short, communication becomes a planned part of the management process.[5]

NIPPING A CRISIS "IN THE BUD"

A recent experience at Federal Express demonstrates how a proactive approach can produce excellent results. By moving aggressively ahead of a crisis to get the facts to employees concerning an upcoming ABC network show, Federal Express defused a potentially explosive situation.

According to Tom Martin, managing director of employee communications, Federal Express had that opportunity in 1989 when ABC's "20/20" TV program planned to feature a negative report based almost entirely on information supplied by a disgruntled employee.

The report centered around the company's alleged poor performance on its "Constant Surveillance Service" (CSS). This is a higher-cost service which requires that the document being shipped remain in the courier's hands or sight all the time. As Martin pointed out:

> The government's investigation (because government shipments were involved) found paperwork errors in less than one percent of the shipments, a margin of error which government officials found acceptable. However, the "20/20" report failed to mention the government's findings. It confused the CSS service with the handling of restricted articles and even alleged rampant drug use by FedEx employees. No government people or experts were quoted.

Point-Counterpoint

Federal Express scheduled a special interactive show on its satellite TV network the same day "20/20" was to air. Executive Vice President Jim Barksdale, plus executives from sales, legal and employee communications, explained the situation and answered as many questions as possible during the 1-hour show. Thirty-five questions were called in, most of them from rank-and-file employees. Martin gave this summary:

[5]Roger D'Aprix, "Communicators in Contemporary Organizations," from *Inside Organizational Communication,* edited by Carol Reuss and Donn Silvis, p. 29. Copyright © 1985 by Longman Publishing Group. Reprinted by permission of Longman Publishing Group.

Because of this preemptive action, employees rallied in support of the company. After the program aired, employees helped deliver thousands of letters to customers explaining the company's position. As a result, customer calls ran ninety percent favorable and there were no negative follow-up stories in the external media.

This represents an excellent example of how an in-house TV network can be used to defuse potentially negative situations—with punctuality and candor—thus letting employees in on the news at or before the time it is covered by the external media.

POSITIONING THE FUNCTION

Among the more popular subjects at professional meetings are the questions about where employee communication should be located on the organization chart and about how to staff the activity, particularly at the local level in multi-plant organizations.

How these questions are answered will have a definite effect on how effectively the function can operate.

Ideally, the employee communication function should answer directly to the chief executive officer of the company, division, plant or office—if the goal is to have this function exercise the greatest degree of independent thinking and actions for top management consideration. It makes sense to remove layers of authority as well as the inevitable involvement of screening and politics. Lower-level positioning of this function weakens the employee communication thrust because it is then regarded as just another constituency of public relations or employee relations.

Reporting to the top can be a disadvantage, too, if the communicator is perceived as operating out of the CEO's office—and as a result, information flow to him or her is also perceived to be filtered or withheld.

From a practical standpoint, as a corporate staff function, the employee communication director should report to the vice president for public relations or personnel. At group, division, plant or staff levels, the communicator should report to the ranking executive of the organization. Regular access to the CEO and to all but the most proprietary of information should be standard operating procedure.

The employee communication function deserves a top-level position—not because it looks good on the organization chart or inflates the ego. Whether we like it or not, the organizational hierarchy establishes ranks of prestige and authority and that translates into recognition, respect, access and power. And those are valuable resources for getting things done in any organization.

Beyond what the organizational chart bestows, the internal communication function—if done well—has real power in providing an effective communication link between top management and the entire employee group. And the more effective the function, the greater self-power it generates.

STAFFING THE FUNCTION

One of the most frequent questions from students is what qualifications are most important for people entering the employee communication field. In evaluating candidates for employee communication positions, it is important to establish high standards both in terms of education and experience.

It is absolutely essential that candidates know how to write well. Virtually every creative activity in the public relations or mass-communication fields has its genesis in clear, concise and interesting writing. Yet, in my experience, this has been one of the most common failings in college graduates looking for careers in the field.

A solid liberal arts and communication foundation should be strengthened with courses in behavioral psychology, business and government. Students also should aggressively seek writing experiences while attending college—and especially during summer periods when the work can be full-time. The more basic, varied and tough the writing experience, the better.

It is highly important for the communicator, once employed, to work hard to secure a broad-based understanding of the organization, its objectives, power sources and politics—as well as how major sections operate and what the employees expect from a communication program. This is especially critical for someone coming to an organization "from the outside," and it calls for an aggressive "learning mode" from the first day on the job. A sincere sensitivity to human values and the ability to develop effective human networks of associates are also important.

In addition to the usual requirements of brains and a healthy work ethic, people who expect to succeed in this field also should have tenacity and a dogged determination. Newcomers will be working in a field which has not yet earned its full spurs at most companies, and they will find plenty of challenges and opportunities in seeking to do an outstanding job with the challenges and opportunities increasing with the size and complexity of the organization.

CENTRALIZATION VERSUS DECENTRALIZATION

Some communication executives favor further decentralization of corporate activities while strengthening group/division/plant/office/warehouse communication systems. While such proposals might give a first-glance promise of hefty reductions in staff costs, they also pose some serious dangers to the operation of an effective company-wide internal communication system.

Few can argue with the need to strengthen communication activities at the group, division, plant or office levels in multi-location companies. But to do so at the expense of a cost-effective corporate coordinating function would be foolish. In the long run, it would also be detrimental to a sound understanding of corporate goals, objectives and problems by all employees, regardless of where they work.

Who Speaks for the Corporation?

No single unit—such as major operating groups or business units—can speak for the entire corporate enterprise. There are compelling reasons for maintaining a strong, cost-effective system for expressing corporate thinking, actions and plans—as well as for maintaining an effective network to ensure proper distribution of these messages to outlying locations.

No company can leave these important responsibilities to chance or to the judgment of dozens of independent local units, which often may push local priorities at the expense of those of the corporate enterprise. From the viewpoint of the corporate communication manager, it is not a matter of controlling local operations. Rather, the purpose is to help local units achieve a reasonable balance between corporate and local information—with full recognition of the priorities of both—and to manage this service-coordination responsibility to the maximum benefit of both.

OPERATING IN MULTI-LOCATION ORGANIZATIONS

In organizations which have many separate operations, it is fundamentally important to hire a competent manager or coordinator at each location to be responsible for the local communication effort and to be the distribution point for corporate materials.

The employee communication manager in facilities of 1,000 or more people should be a full-time, well-trained and experienced professional. In smaller operations, the communication manager should be capable of handling both internal and external communication.

He or she should be a member of the unit manager's staff, somebody who attends staff meetings with full observer rights— plus full participation rights in all discussions relating to the broad aspects of communication. There are some who say local communicators should not be allowed to sit in on "high councils" of the organization; they add that these people usually do not have adequate qualifications to assume such responsibilities.

The fact that this is unfortunately true in many cases is an indictment of established hierarchies and of the traditional manager's low respect for the communication function. If a top-flight communication job is the goal, a qualified professional communicator needs to be appointed and given the authority, access to information and decision-making responsibilities required to carry out the assignment properly.

In the quest for successful three-way communication systems, the sideways flow of information is usually the toughest to achieve. The Japanese emphasize cross-communication through a combination of the teamwork approach and consensus decision making, plus full sharing of information among various departments.

It is at the staff level that lateral communication has to be firmly established, practiced and enforced if it is to achieve an integral system of three-way communication. As a full-fledged participant in staff activities, the employee communication manager can help to organize and execute all aspects needed for three-way communication.

CORPORATE SERVICES FOR LOCAL OPERATIONS

For multi-location organizations, it is strongly recommended that the company's central office coordinate and assist local communication activities. Here are some basic services which should be considered:

Operation of a daily newsline. Using telephones or electronic transmission and covering important company and industry news, the newsline can be used in local communication activities. This is the best buy in the communication arsenal.

Distribution of weekly or semi-monthly "syndicated" print and graphic materials. These materials will allow for direct inserts or adaptation with local information.

Establishment of publication guidelines. These guidelines should include a mission statement and general goals for all company publications.

Development of annual "information priorities." This can serve as a unifying core on key issues—to be supplemented and localized at each installation.

Annual conference for editors and communicators. This conference can feature talks by key company executives, as well as skills-training workshops manned by the firm's best communicators. This is particularly critical when the local communication function is handled by employees without professional training and experience, who do this job part time.

Awards for publication excellence. These could be featured at each year's communicators' conference.

Other possibilities. An editor's notebook, one which discusses basic philosophy, plus fundamental rules in such areas as writing, pictures, layout, approval systems and cost savings, could be considered. Also, a publication evaluation service is another possibility, although this can be very time consuming.

REASONS COMMUNICATORS GIVE FOR NOT COMMUNICATING AGGRESSIVELY

Here are a dozen reasons/excuses that communicators often give for why they don't (can't) communicate well with employees:

1. Management doesn't understand or support communication.

2. I could never get that kind of story approved; we've never done it before.

3. Somebody up high always wants to fuzzy-up stories so that bad news is camouflaged or eliminated.

4. There are too many union objections.

5. The media relations department usually decides what we say to employees — also when and how.

6. I am hindered by a lack of access to top-level information.

7. Legal restrictions make it difficult for us to tell the whole story.

8. Special communication for managers is bad; it creates a "we-they" situation.

9. I don't have all the facts yet; let's wait until all the i's are dotted and t's are crossed before we say anything.

10. There's not enough money.

11. There's not enough people or time.

12. We can't prove bottom-line value.

SUMMARY

Some employee communication programs are like swat
an outdoor barbecue: a lot of flailing around, a few hit
many accomplishments to write home about.

Establishment of an on-going, reliable and respected i.   .nal communication process should be a priority goal. It takes a lot of serious thought, as well as cooperation from key people in several staffs and at various levels of the organization. The system needs to be considered in the context of an overall strategic plan, one with short- and long-range goals, regular evaluations and a commitment to make employee communication a valuable management resource.

Closer ties between employee communication functions and line management will expand its value to the organization and, in turn, strengthen the communication process as a facilitator of constructive change.

The ideal is to get communicators to think, plan and execute like managers and to be aggressive in persuading managers to think and act more like communicators.

The goal is not a program of fly swatting or isolated responses to events and calamities, but a carefully thought-out plan of action based on sound professional and moral principles. What is needed is an on-going process which makes its contributions day-in and day-out, building strength and respect as it does so—qualities that will help the process survive both good times and bad.

CASE 4

Saginaw Division, General Motors

MODEL SYSTEM FOR DIVERSE
COMMUNICATION NEEDS

Saginaw Division is the largest of ten component-manufacturing divisions within GM's Automotive Components Group. It employs 14,000 people, largely in twenty-three office and plant sites in North America, England and Spain, and in sales offices in Europe. The division produces steering components and drive axles for GM vehicle divisions and many non-GM customers all over the world.

In 1981, when Ron Actis became director of public affairs,* he inherited an employee communication program which was practically nonexistent. Over the next 6 years, he constructed step-by-step what corporate communication executives regarded as the most effective total communication system in General Motors.

Previously, the division's only formal communication with employees was a daily one-page newsletter published and posted at divisional offices and faxed to outlying sites in Athens, Ala.; Buffalo, N.Y.; and Detroit, Mich. The majority of articles dealt with the auto industry and General Motors, but they contained very little divisional information.

RESEARCH SHOWED MAJOR DEFICIENCIES

Initial research revealed:

- Poor communication throughout the division, a lack of trust between management and unions, decision making limited to a handful of people, minimum employee involvement and unpredictable leadership.
- In general, a lack of employee awareness of the division's mission, successes and failures.
- Employees felt that divisional executives were isolated and out of touch with the work force.

---
*
In 1987, Actis became director of public affairs for GM's Automotive Components Group.

- Middle management usually received information at th or after it was given to the union.

- Supervisors received little more than production sc... safety-related information.

Actis embarked on a sizable undertaking to build a modern internal communication system for Saginaw Division—with the strong support of the division's top management.

Actis' vision for Saginaw Division was to establish what he called a "synchronous communication" plan. It was to be a process which gets the right message to the right audience...at the right time...with the right medium...with progress measured on a continuous basis. It was to be a two-way process—listening as well as talking—among all levels of the organization, a process designed to build employee trust and confidence in the division's management.

To ensure top-level interest, support and ownership, the general managers' staff became a Communications Advisory Committee, which met monthly to review progress and problems and to offer suggestions for improving the communication program.

DIVERSIFIED PLAN

The divisional plan had five specific goals:

1. To strengthen print communication with employees and the total manager-supervisory group.
2. To reinforce print communication using regular videotapes.
3. To establish special "rifle-shot" publications to improve union and supplier relations as well as top management's awareness of key public issues affecting the business.
4. To greatly increase face-to-face dialogue between division executives, plant supervisors and employees.
5. To continuously evaluate all communication processes to achieve maximum effectiveness.

The plan involved a number of fundamental steps:

- To educate executives on what internal communication can accomplish in terms of bottom-line business results.
- To increase divisional business news in the *Daily Newsletter* to at least seventy-five percent of total content.

- To publish a monthly tabloid entitled *Steering Columns* to provide all employees with more in-depth business information about divisional issues and activities.
- To launch a new bi-monthly *Report to Supervisors,* a two-page newsletter for supervisors which could also be used in face-to-face sessions with their employees.

Saginaw Division also established four publications with limited purpose and circulation aimed at important segments of the division's "family" public:

- *Dialog,* to assist plant editors around the world.
- *Insight,* to provide news on government issues to upper levels of management.
- *Joint Activities,* to improve management and labor interaction.
- *21st Century Supplier,* to elicit supplier support in achieving divisional business goals.

Once the print side of the plan was in place, the division launched a quarterly video newsmagazine, shown to employees on company time. These videos featured confidential information through interviews with management, union officials, employees, customers and suppliers. The videos promote face-to-face discussions between supervisors and employees on such important matters as quality, customer satisfaction and cost reduction.

FACE-TO-FACE COMMUNICATION

The plan also called for an increase in regular face-to-face meetings involving the division's top managers. The general manager spearheaded a series of "no-holds-barred" meetings with employees that convinced him that the division should formalize increased employee meetings involving members of the division staff. This involved seventeen scheduled communication meetings a month, covering all business areas and including all types of employees as well as union officials.

For example, a general manager-employee meeting takes place at one of the division's domestic plants each month on a rotating basis. Bimonthly, there's a a question-and-answer session between the plant manager, the plant staff and volunteers from various production departments. There are annual meetings for top-divisional executives, middle management and all supervisors.

COMPREHENSIVE EVALUATION PROCESS

The final critical element in Saginaw Division's communication effort is a comprehensive evaluation process. Actis believes the true test of any communication activity must involve measurement of its effectiveness and its impact on the target audience. Regular evaluations have provided valuable information on how to strengthen various communication activities.

Saginaw Division also has conducted studies on information flow and the responsiveness of employees to product quality goals established by the division. Both studies revealed a number of deficiencies to which increased attention was directed.

Saginaw Division is confident it's on the right track.

What's the bottom line?

The 1982 communication audit showed that employees were not satisfied with the communication process, that they were left out of the information loop, and that less than half of the division's employees believed management information. In a 1986 study, most employees believed that management was doing a good job communicating with them. And management's credibility soared to eighty percent—a high rating for large industrial organizations.

Chapter 4

Manager's Role in the Communication Process: The Frozen Middle Syndrome

Since the early 1980s, increasing attention has been given by some businesses to communicating more effectively with their management groups. There are a number of reasons for this new direction.

Research in the mid-1980s began to point directly to the middle-management group as a serious obstacle to effective communication. This research led to the discovery of the so-called "frozen middle" syndrome, the inability or reluctance of lower- and middle-management people to pass information along—upward, downward or laterally. However, any reasoned analysis must include the first-level supervisors, too, if the most critical areas in the communication process are to be properly evaluated.

FEW COMPANIES HAVE ALL-OUT ATTACKS

The whole subject of information sharing with management poses one of the biggest paradoxes in employee communication.

Virtually every study shows that the most effective, the most desired and the most reliable source of communication with the total employee group is the employee's immediate supervisor. This is the vital link for two-way communication, where employees and their ideas and concerns can be blended with the downward flow of information to produce a dynamic, productive interaction.

Yet few companies have really launched all-out attacks designed to make the entire management group a truly effective communication network.

MISTRUST AND LACK OF CONFIDENCE IN SENIOR MANAGEMENT

Better bonding of senior corporate executives with the rest of the management group in basic understanding and philosophy is a critical need in the battle to meet world competition. Yet, research shows glaring deficiencies, if not deterioration, in the teamwork relationship between top management and the supervisory group.

A 1989 study of 400 managers and professionals conducted by Robert Kelley,[1] business professor at the Carnegie Mellon University, revealed serious mistrust and lack of confidence in the skills and vision of senior executives.

Here are key findings:

- Nearly two thirds of the respondents said their company's leadership failed to insure "a clear understanding of a corporate vision, mission and goals" among members of its work force.

- Only about one in five company executives were identified as having the skills to "motivate employees and to implement a vision successfully enough to result in high performance results."

- Only one in three workers feels "tied into the company's destiny" and its performance goals.

- Ninety-five percent of the managers said they could be more productive, but nearly two-thirds said management failed to capitalize on their ideas and efforts about half the time.

- The Carnegie Mellon study also showed that only 42 percent of the managers were identified as being able to instill trust in their subordinates.

- The respondents said they trust their top management only about 55 percent of the time.

[1] Robert E. Kelley, news release on "Gold Collar Worker Survey," issued by Carnegie Mellon University, November 9, 1989.

It is worth noting that in all of these deficiencies in the management environment of American business, open two-way communication could have made significant improvements — in communicating the organization's vision and goals, in recognizing and using employee ideas, in building trust and in motivating employees to higher levels of performance.

WHY SUPERVISORS RATE POORLY

Why do supervisors come out so poorly when judged for their communication performance?   Lack of a regular, meaty flow of information *to* them, as well as *from* them, is high on the list. So are skills training and time to communicate. Also important is the all-too-frequent lack of reward incentives for doing a good job.

Increases in the time and incentives for supervisors to communicate are beyond the normal responsibilities of communicators. But communicators certainly should keep hammering away at these goals with higher management at every opportunity.

However, information flow and skills training *are* prime responsibilities of communication managers. Even though the training function may be located elsewhere on the company's organization chart, the communication manager should be aggressive in advancing training activities to improve communication skills of all management people.

Managers, particularly first-line supervisors, need good background and reasons for management actions—the information necessary to respond to employee questions. All employees deserve to know more than just what the decisions are. They also want to know the "whys" and "whats"—why the decisions were made and what they mean to employees and their jobs.

We must be careful not to put all the blame for poor communication in American business and industry on first- and second-level supervisors. As a matter of fact, from a selfish standpoint, if nothing else, most managers do want to communicate honestly and openly with their employees. Higher performance can be achieved in an environment where everyone knows the mission and also understands his or her own role in getting the job done right.

Now, with companies pushing decision making down to the lowest possible levels, lower-and middle-level managers are forced to use their new-found freedom to take independent action. But some are not sure they want to take the risk involved; a mistake could reflect badly on their career charts. As a result, many managers feel out of their "comfort zone" and are inclined to be indecisive in trying new paths.

"NOBODY TOLD US THAT WAS OUR JOB"

Also, some first- and second-level supervisors defend their inaction by saying, "Nobody ever told us that was our job." In addition, some higher-level executives are reluctant to provide sensitive information to first-line supervisors because many supervisors came from hourly ranks where they were union members. This, the critics say, can give them divided loyalties and open a possible pipeline of inside information to union headquarters.

In one Midwestern company, about half of the first- and second-level supervisors, when queried, asked to be removed from the mailing list for the company's management publication. They couldn't relate corporate philosophy and priorities to their own jobs, and they said they didn't have time to read anything at work that wasn't directly related to their jobs. But they did want more information about their own local operations where the relevance was more obvious and where the information helped them to do their jobs.

Perhaps even more significant—if you follow the half-full, half-empty glass theory—more than half of the managers *did* want the company's management publication. That's a reasonably good level of interest among lower-level supervisors in having the corporate line.

FIRST-LINE SUPERVISOR AN UNLIKELY CHOICE

One of my professional associates made an interesting point in a professionals' round-table discussion about the role of first-line supervisors when he questioned whether the primary responsibility for communication should be higher up in the organization.

Mike Emanuel, who heads his own New York-based consulting firm, said:

> First-line supervisors are the least-likely managers to be good communicators when it comes to the non-job-related information that

corporate management wants distributed—things like company performance, competition, profitability and public issues. They are loaded up with too many jobs to handle. They're not tied into the organization's regular information flow.

Our most recent surveys show them to be the unhappiest of all supervisors, sometimes even more than hourly employees. Most complain to us that they have difficulty explaining subjects such as complicated profit-sharing formulas or financial data. And we don't reward or promote them for being good communicators. Without considerable help and adequate resources, it's unrealistic to expect them to also be good communicators. What is needed are some dramatic changes in their entire job structure and the philosophy of what a supervisor is.

"FROZEN MIDDLE" OR "FROZEN TOP"?

Serious questions also are being raised about whether the communication bottleneck is with first- and second-level supervisors or is actually higher on the organizational chart. In a corporate structure, for example, vice presidents and their immediate subordinates set the climate and example for their managerial group; in plants, it's the plant manager and his or her staff.

At General Electric, the phrase "cement layer" is used to describe the middle-management that resists change—and block information exchange. But GE Chairman John F. Welch disagrees.

> Communication often breaks down in areas of the organization where the impact of change is felt most. I've seen it happen, literally, at the very top of some businesses. No level of management has a monopoly on cement, and to make middle management synonymous with a cement layer is a bad rap—and inaccurate.[2]

Charging Up the Hill

It is true that when the top people really want something like communication to happen, it usually does—and vice versa. But not always!

For example, Chairman Roger Smith wanted all General Motors employees to understand the need for the massive changes he believed were necessary to ensure future world leadership for his

[2] The employee publication of General Electric, *Monogram*, (Fall 1989), p. 4.

company. But he was surprised and sorely disappointed when it didn't happen, particularly with the management group.

When *Fortune* asked Smith in 1989 what he would do differently—if he could—in the way he went about making changes to modernize GM after he became CEO in 1981, he said:

> I'd make exactly the same decisions. I'd begin to rebuild General Motors, inside out and from the bottom up, to turn it into a 21st-century corporation, one that would continue to be a global leader.
>
> But, I sure wish I'd done a better job of communicating with GM people. I'd do that differently a second time around and make sure they understood and shared my vision for the company. Then they would have known why I was tearing the place up, taking out whole divisions, changing our whole production structure. I never got all this across.
>
> There we were, charging up the hill right on schedule, and I looked behind me and saw that many people were still at the bottom, trying to decide whether to come along. I'm talking about hourly workers, middle management, even some top managers. It seemed like a lot of them had gotten off the train. [3]

MAJOR CHANGES WITHIN GM SYSTEM

Clearly, ineffective communication on the huge changes taking place was GM's most serious communication failure during the 1980s. At best, it was a formidable assignment.

Ineffective communication on huge changes was GM's most serious communication failure during the 1980s.

Elimination of long-time major divisions, massive changes in organizational structure, elimination of eleven large manufacturing plants, heavy cuts in personnel, major acquisitions, mergers and joint ventures with foreign competitors—all became symbols of the new GM. But it was a new GM which employees found difficult to

[3] Roger B. Smith, "The U.S. Must Do As GM Has Done," FORTUNE, February 13, 1989, p. 71.

understand. There were too many major changes that they didn't understand and couldn't relate to their own personal job potential and security.

Failure to communicate effectively on the acquisition of Electronic Data Systems, Inc., was perhaps the most detrimental in terms of lack of understanding and negative effect on employee morale. The EDS experience magnified the trauma of employees and management alike, a trauma resulting from the unprecedented changes underway in the giant corporation. In the process, employee confidence, loyalty, commitment and trust suffered damage that would take years to restore.

The blame for ineffective communication during this difficult period, of course, has to be shared by a lot of GM management people. And there were communicators who fought hard for more aggressive, open communication concerning the changes taking place, but obviously weren't as persuasive as they should have been.

D'Aprix believes the negative effects of massive reorganizational changes of the 80's will be felt for decades.

> Careless and insensitive corporate downsizing across America has left us with at least one workplace generation of fear, anger, ill will and mistrust. Restructuring is a reasonable business value, but when it gets translated into something that conflicts with human values, you're going to have serious problems in employee communication and employee relations.

MAKING A MERGER TRANSITION EASIER

When Federal Express acquired the Flying Tigers organization in 1989, it carried out a strong, multi-faceted communication effort covering worldwide operations of both organizations. This program included almost daily coverage over the FedEX satellite TV network, four live broadcasts, a "welcome aboard" video for the new employees and strong coverage in the company's publications.

Tom Martin, who directs employee communication activities at Federal Express, says the "Joining Forces" communication program "gave employees of both companies a better understanding of the merger and made the transition period a lot easier on everyone." (For more information on the merger communication effort, see Case Example 11 on Federal Express at the end of Chapter 8.)

MASSIVE CHANGES IN SUPERVISOR'S JOB?

The goal of strengthening the position of front-line supervisors is much bigger than just the communication function. It raises questions about the stature that American business and industry in general bestows on—and the confidence it feels in—the first- and second-level supervisors.

Are businesses taking full advantage of the people in this group as catalysts/leaders in motivating higher performance and loyalty, in stimulating new ideas? Or are they so loaded with problems of production quality and quantity, absenteeism, union grievances and other administrative duties that they have neither the time nor the incentives to carry out the higher elements of leadership? Do businesses look on supervisors as production and paper clerks rather than as team leaders for the total management process?

For a long time, typical industrial supervisors have had two basic priorities drummed into their heads: "Get the iron out the door and don't go over your budget." In recent years, product quality has been added to this list, and strongly enforced. When you add safety and labor grievances, absenteeism problems and a few other headaches that absolutely must be dealt with on a daily basis, it's not hard to see why the communication aspects of a supervisor's job seldom get done—at least not the way they should be done.

MANAGERS MUST SEE PAYOFF

How do we motivate managers, at all levels, to do a better job of communicating?

It's as simple as this: If managers can't see a payoff for themselves in the communication assignment, the job won't get done. If managers, from CEO to first-line supervisor, don't believe there is a hard-cash payoff for them—in the paycheck, in bonuses or in promotions—communication becomes just another low-priority job that goes on the shelf in the closet without a light.

At the same time, all managers need to do is look at recent research in this field to see that almost invariably, when managers are perceived by their employees as leaders who sincerely practice open, honest, two-way communication, they are also rated by their subordinates as being more effective managers. Good communication and leadership go hand-in-hand.

Fortunately, there is a strong movement in industrial companies to give serious study to the shape and form of the supervisory function in light of changing job demands and work cultures. One fundamental change enjoying increasing popularity is the use of hourly, unionized employees as team leaders. These team leaders are put in charge of four-to-ten employees to promote teamwork, camaraderie and union support. Some call them "self-directed" work groups or teams. Several teams report to a group leader or salaried supervisor, whose role involves more leadership, encouragement and help than is typically encountered in the traditional, authoritarian context of managing.

The Japanese do this exceptionally well, and many American companies are also using it very successfully. In organizations using this business-team approach, there are strong pressures to keep the hourly team leaders fully informed about the business—a sharp departure from past practices of industrial America.

MANY SMALL IMPROVEMENTS ARE THE KEY

When American business executives cite examples of progress, they are inclined to talk about things like huge building projects, massive reorganizations, new lines of innovative products or new technology. But the greatest gains in productivity by far come from a continual stream of relatively small improvements—on a day-to-day basis—in every part of the organization. They come from employees who know the business, are given the facts they need to probe for better mousetraps, and a management team receptive to new ideas—including some that are "off the wall."

Mark Potts and Peter Behr in *The Leading Edge* point out that some companies have found that there are people in their organizations—working with little attention for years—who have a creative overdrive that can be turned on if the right conditions are established.

> Companies must establish a conduit for ideas—from product proposals to suggestions for smaller improvements—that allows innovation to surface easily, without having to battle up through the layers of bureaucracy. We need to open the avenues of communication for projects that may sound slightly out of the corporate culture.[4]

[4] Mark Potts and Peter Behr, *The Leading Edge* (New York: McGraw-Hill Publishing Co., 1987), p. 133.

GM's Bob Stramy points out the striking contrast in employee involvement in the Japanese and American auto industries, showing that seventy percent of all Japanese employees are involved in decision making. This figure compares to about twelve percent in U.S. auto companies—mostly higher-level employees. Studies also show that the average worker at Toyota, Nissan and Honda auto plants submits twenty-seven improvement suggestions a year, with ninety percent implementation. This compares with only one suggestion for every thirty-seven American auto workers, with only twenty percent implemented.[5]

The dramatic changes which have taken place in American business since the early 1980s have placed a higher premium on informed, loyal employees. Parker Hannifin's Dick Charlton says:

> In the restructured, streamlined plant and office staffs of today, layers of management have often been removed, placing greater responsibility on the individual worker. If an employee is not informed and loyal, and does not exercise initiative and good judgment, the company may sustain immense damage before problems are spotted and corrected.[6]

BALANCE OF TEAMWORK AND INDIVIDUAL EFFORT

The battle for survival and success comes—in business as in wars—from people in the front-line trenches, i.e., with good first-line supervisors (or team leaders) getting maximum performance and improvement ideas from their people. Maximum achievement, at this level particularly, requires a skillful balance of teamwork and individual effort—one which optimizes group accomplishment while still energizing the entrepreneurial drive for new ideas.

If the supervisor is an SOB, all the effective communication in the world won't make him an effective leader.

---

[5] Robert J. Stramy, John J. Nora and C. Raymond Rogers' *Transforming the Work Place* (Princeton, N.J.: Princeton Research Institute, 1986), p. 4.

[6] Richard G. Charlton, "The Decade of the Employee," Public Relations Journal (January 1990), p. 26.

This kind of teamwork success formula works only in a climate of belief—one of demonstrated proof that management welcomes upward communication, tolerates whistle blowers, and responds to suggestions and concerns. If the supervisor is an SOB, all the effective communication in the world won't make him an effective leader of people and a stimulator of ideas.

Tom Peters, in *Thriving on Chaos,* says:

> One of the distinguishing characteristics of the best leaders is their personal thirst for and continuing quest for new/small/practical ideas...Everyone, in every function must constantly pursue innovation; the average firm's overall capacity for innovation must increase dramatically.
>
> The Japanese have created a corporate capacity for innovation...In contrast, American industry treats our workers like rote executors. And our first-line supervisors, too. We even treat our middle managers as administrators—not creators of new and constantly improving order.[7]

Significant changes may be required if the first- and second-level supervisors are to have more effective roles in leading their people to higher levels of performance and more cooperative attitudes toward management and their jobs.

MANAGERS "LEFT OUT IN THE COLD"

Over the years, many companies have systematically excluded a majority of the people in their manager-supervisor group from a regular flow of important company information, based on archaic tradition and elitist thinking. Managers have the right to stand up and say to top management, as one GM plant superintendent did, "We didn't want to be your frozen middle. But you left us out in the cold."

The typical response of top executives in the past went something like this: "We tell them what they need to know. If we gave them detailed business information, they wouldn't know how to use it anyway." Then top management is shocked when their troops

---

[7] Tom Peters, *Thriving on Chaos* (New York: Random House, 1987), p. 277.

don't rally enthusiastically to the company bugle call for "charge" and don't even know the words to the fight songs they are supposed to sing.

This is not to fault anyone particularly. It's the way autocratic systems worked in the not-too-distant past—and worked very well for those times. But they could have worked better. And now the modern management system *must* work better if American businesses expect to secure maximum cooperation and performance from their employees.

AFTER SMOKE OF BATTLE CLEARS AWAY

Times are changing. In 1988, a major manufacturing company located in the Northeast was faced with the unsettling prospects of a hostile takeover by a conglomerate. In response, the company made extensive organizational changes and redirected its business and research resources to improve efficiency and to focus more resources on high-potential product areas.

The firm desperately wanted its employees to know the facts behind the takeover bid and what it could mean to them. Communication activities were beefed up—including a special newsletter which was published twice a month. But the most dramatic communication action was the establishment of a weekly conference of the company's 250 management executives to discuss the company's problems, as well as actions being taken or considered.

After the smoke of the takeover battle clears away, will this company make full use of this new-found communication tool? Will it use this group—in monthly or even quarterly sessions—to forge a strong communication link between company management and all employees, using the 250-member management group as its linkage?

More often than not, a company under siege from antagonists outside corporate walls, will leave its inner flanks exposed. And that's when full support from its own troops is most critical. Or after the battle is won—and the smoke drifts away—so does support for the internal communication program that worked so well in time of crisis.

REASONS MANAGERS GIVE
FOR NOT COMMUNICATING WELL

Here are a dozen reasons/excuses managers give for why they don't (can't) communicate well.

1. The information will get into the hands of competitors or the news media.

2. Employees can't understand reasons for management decisions, particularly bad news.

3. I believe in the "need-to-know" principle. Why do they have to know anything except how to do their own jobs?

4. I don't have the time.

5. I'm not really good at talking to employees.

6. I don't trust my employees to handle sensitive information properly.

7. Too risky. I got burned once when I tried to be honest with my employees, so never again.

8. There's not enough money.

9. Information is power, and I'm not giving it away.

10. My managers don't give me any information to communicate.

11. Top management will never let us tell the whole truth, particularly if it has negative aspects.

12. There's a lack of consistency in communicating; I don't know what I'm expected to do.

SUPERVISOR-EMPLOYEE COMMUNICATION LINK

And how does the supervisor view his or her role in being the most important link in an organization's communication process?

One of the most frequent reasons managers give for not communicating is: "I just don't have time." That's probably true for a majority of supervisors who must manage their time and set hard-nosed priorities to survive—let alone succeed. But because the process of communication is so basic to almost every aspect of a manager's job, it cannot be viewed as just another part of his or her job. (For a candid view of what a front-line manufacturing manager in a 2700-employee business expects from his communicator, see Case Example 5 on GM's Glenn Reeser at the end of this chapter, pages 100-103.)

Successful managers look at communication as a strong thread for weaving various aspects of the job together effectively. It's not something extra—it's the essence of leadership. If they push the communication job aside until they find time, it will seldom get done.

The ideal communication relationship between manager and employees starts with the job itself.

Employees want and need to know things like: "What is my job?" "How am I doing?" "How can I contribute more?" "Will my boss evaluate my work fairly?" Most employees also want to know the broader picture, such as: "What are the challenges and goals of the whole operation?" "How does our group fit in with others in our plant, office or department?" "Who are our organization's chief competitors and how are we doing against them?" Simply put, employees want the boss to share important information with them and to trust them.

But the supervisor-worker communication relationship involves more than just information about the business. There is a deeply-rooted desire by employees to have the boss show an interest in them as individuals and in such off-the-job priorities as family and community service—and even how the golf game went over the weekend.

This broad approach to supervisory communication helps employees feel a sense of value, of belonging to the organization. Such interest assures employees that their own security is probably okay as long as they continue doing a good job. It builds respect among employees for a boss who is interested in them as human beings— both on and off the job. This is why good managers spend a lot of time "wandering around" among their people rather than being chained to administrative chores behind a desk.

Sharing, a sense of belonging, trust, respect, sincere personal interest and frequent face-to-face contact—those are powerful basics on which to build a strong, trusting and productive relationship, one held together and strengthened by communication.

Management Communication Has Broad Appeal

The idea of beefing up the management communication system should have great appeal not only for professional communicators but for front-line supervisors as well. Supplying all managers with more important business information will obviously make them more knowledgeable and understanding members of the management team—and presumably make them more effective as leaders.

In addition, they can be a valuable conduit for the dissemination of information to the employees they supervise. And the total management communication process, if done properly, can provide unity, direction and a stronger sense of ownership to the entire management group.

Unfortunately, an open, pervasive communication philosophy is too often stated but seldom enforced or practiced. It is unrealistic to believe that this goal can be achieved unless top management's commitment is made perfectly clear and is believed by the total management group.

Only through repetition—in strategic plans, at management conferences, in talks to management and employee groups and in press conferences—will the goal become a reality. Only by making good communication a key element in the promotion and reward systems will it become standard practice. Only when top company executives demonstrate open communication by example will the rest of the management organization believe and follow suit.

At Johnson & Johnson, the manager has an unusually heavy responsibility for the company's internal communication effort because there is no direct communication to nonmanagement employees from the corporate level. The company is highly decentralized, and each major group within the company is expected to conduct its own formal and informal communication activities, making use of corporate information which local managers feel fits into their communication plans.

As Larry Foster, public relations vice president, says:

> We consider our managers an important part of the total communication effort, representing the corporation to their employees and to the community, and we strive to impart information to them on a timely basis. This information is designed to help them better understand the most significant events and business-building opportunities which exist within the corporation; and to help them in carrying out their business responsibilities and enhancing their own careers as well.

HELPING MANAGERS COMMUNICATE BETTER

Here is a brief checklist of other ways in which higher management can contribute to helping managers become better communicators—by giving support, recognition and credibility to this responsibility.

1. Encourage downward, upward and lateral communication by all managers and supervisors as a means of stimulating a continuing flow of good ideas across the entire organization.

2. Provide all managers with a steady flow of relevant corporate information. Management conferences and regular organizational meetings are excellent. But it is important that information shared at these meetings also cascade down to lower layers of supervision, with editorial and visual highlights being extremely helpful in strengthening local meetings. In addition, regular management publications and videotapes should be distributed to the entire management group at each work place—information which managers can share with their employees on the job.

3. Local management should provide additional relevant business information to its supervisors about their own local operation, showing how this operation contributes to and benefits from corporate activities, and how it directly affects local employees. Important information could be supplied to supervisors through daily reports on highlights of staff meetings, weekly summaries of comments from the plant manager explaining actions or discussing current and proposed plans, and/or quarterly

15-minute videotapes for use by first-level supervisors at regular meetings with their people.

4.   Provide special training to all supervisors on the importance of effective communication in managing their jobs, and also provide skills training in real life situations to help them be better communicators on the job.

5.   Make good communication a fundamental element in the promotion and rewards systems.

To be truly effective, this can't just be a sentence in a policy letter or a part of the hymns we sing about things like motherhood, apple pie and communication. It deserves more than a pat on the back and a few kind words. Communication must be a leadership asset, one which is included as a separate item on manager appraisals and used as a key factor in determining salary raises, promotions and bonus awards.

COMMUNICATION VITAL TO LEADERSHIP

Management policy and practice should make it clear that a person can't be a good manager—an effective leader—unless he or she communicates well.

If we expect managers to be a primary source of information for employees, it follows that they must be on the primary network for corporate and local business information. In many companies, traditional practices exclude all but the highest level executives from more important information. Recent surveys indicate that top managements are sharing more information with the people in their supervisory group and that more of this information is being passed along to their employees.

In 1987–89 surveys conducted at seventeen different companies by Towers, Perrin, Forster and Crosby, about two-thirds of the employees said their supervisors kept them well informed and nearly seventy percent said their supervisors were kept well informed by higher management. The TPF&C studies also showed that levels of satisfaction increased with each higher level of management. Or stated another way, satisfaction with information provided decreased with each lower level of management down to the first-level supervisor.

In terms of security, obviously there are types of proprietary information which must be restricted. But common sense evaluation shows that about ninety percent of the information traditionally marked "confidential" is not. And certainly, much of this type of information is very useful to managers.

INCREASING COMMUNICATION ABILITIES OF MANAGERS

Mobilizing the total management group is a formidable undertaking. But the long-range potential of an effective management communication system makes it a priority target for management consideration.

Two areas should be of primary concern to professional communicators: communication training and an increased flow of information.

Communication Training

Many professional communicators—and top executives, too—are inclined to put communication training for the manager-supervisory group far down on their priority lists. The sheer magnitude of numbers, time involvement and costs are major reasons why most large organizations don't have full-scale training programs in this field.

Traditional communicators, who are more comfortable pushing publications, are inclined to say: "Wow, that's a tough assignment that's going to take years of concerted effort before making a real dent. Also, management won't give us enough money to do the job. And besides, that's the training department's responsibility."

My response to those three statements are: "Wrong! Not necessarily! Wrong!"

Training Is Neglected Tool. Communication training for managers is one of the most critical and probably one of the most neglected aspects of industrial training programs for supervisors. And the absence of really effective communication training which is geared for the times has a very negative effect on many broad-based employee communication programs. If you don't believe it, conduct some focus-group sessions with various levels of your own supervisory staff. Ask the supervisors what their greatest needs are in terms of helping them be better communicators.

The need for sound communication training is not restricted to front-line managers, but also includes all levels up to the executive suites. Aggressive communication managers should keep training at the top of their priority lists, although it may be somebody else's prime responsibility.

When the question of communication training arises, the normal first response—particularly by training people—is to "pull something off the shelf." They'll probably tell you that communication courses have always been an important part of the basic learning curriculum for managers in your company, particularly for new first-line supervisors.

Take that with a grain of salt! The difference between a traditional communication training session and really effective communication training for management can be as different as night and day. Any course that's been on the shelf more than 5 years probably wouldn't come close to meeting today's needs in most companies. Accelerated change is making obsolete not only traditional management styles, but also stereotyped training packages as well.

Things Unacceptable in Training Plans. Here are several other things you *don't* want in a communication training program:

- Don't bury managers with a master's degree worth of behavioral psychology. Most of them are college graduates, probably with a couple of psychology or related courses under their belts. And if they've been managers for a while, they probably have shop-floor experience equivalent to at least a Ph.D. So, synopsize a few basic principles of human relations as a foundation, and then move on.

- Don't overload them with detailed computer readouts from research to prove the obvious: "Although employees rank their managers as the number one desired source of information, they feel that most of them don't do a very good job." Most managers already know this and similar basic communication facts, anyway. Again, a few highlight facts of life will be plenty.

- Don't let anyone talk you into a week's seminar, or even three days. Managers who need communication training the most are also probably in the most competitive, time-precious aspects of the businesses. Their time is golden, and instructional time off the job must be as compact and productive as possible. One day is best, two days at most—at least for initial sessions, after which evaluations can be made with respect to follow-up training.

How to Ensure Successful Training. What should you expect from training seminars for managers? Here are three basic objectives:

1. To help participants understand the dynamics, basic principles and potential of communication in helping achieve organizational goals.
2. To improve communication skills and confidence of managers.
3. To apply these principles and new skills in discussing possible solutions to practical, on-the-shop-floor or in-the-office problems—and in communicating more effectively about business objectives and issues.

Orient Training to Actual Problems. Here are some additional tips for making training seminars more dynamic and productive—and for making sure their success also contributes to increased support, recognition and respect for the entire internal communication program.

- Pre-seminar research can ascertain the current level of communication proficiency among typical managers and determine their opinions about greatest weaknesses and needs. This knowledge will provide a solid foundation on which to base the substance of the training activity and allow creation of real-life scenarios almost from the beginning.
- The initial training seminar should be a pilot session with veteran managers helping to evaluate and recommend running improvements.

- For maximum benefits, training seminars should be strongly oriented toward actual problems and practical solutions. Seminar participants should have the opportunity to discuss their own toughest problems as a group and to brainstorm together for possible solutions. This allows immediate application of seminar lessons in their own plants or offices and provides positive reinforcement of their value for the managers. Follow-up evaluations and focus-group discussions should be conducted with representative members of the manager group to determine what gains can be credited to the training.
- Employment of outside experts in communication training should be considered—at least for initial sessions within a company and for train-the-trainer activities. Outside counseling firms can bring an extra dimension of experience to the training table, provided the focus is on communicating about the issues of the business.

Emphasize Benefits of Training. To ensure continuing support of special communication training, the communication manager must be sure to emphasize in reports to top management—at both corporate and local levels—two significant benefits which can be expected from effective communication training:

1. *Immediate payoff.* There is an immediate payoff in using the new knowledge, skills and shared experiences of the seminar group, since they can be applied to similar "right-now" problems "back home", problems in which good communication can help produce appropriate solutions.

2. *Long-range benefits.* There are long-range returns in terms of how the new communication knowledge and skills—if strengthened by regular use on the job—can contribute to increased leadership potential for seminar participants in the years ahead. It can definitely make them better managers.

INCREASING INFORMATION FLOW TO MANAGERS

Increasing the flow of information to the total management group is an important responsibility of the employee communication function—at all levels. Among the more important media for communicating broadly with management people are publications, videotapes and satellite television.

It is important to have a clear understanding with top executives when it comes to the goals of management communication. They need to recognize the types of information which will be shared and the benefits of broad distribution. They also need to understand the possibility that some sensitive information may end up in newspapers or magazines, or on radio or TV—and why the potential benefits are much greater than the risks.

These goals and risks should be described in writing, and they should also be discussed face-to-face with top management. Without this kind of understanding, it will be like walking through mine fields every day.

Management Publications

A publication designed exclusively for the entire management-supervisory group gets my vote as a priority communication channel. But it is not an easy task to get top management approval for a channel which carries background information on major company decisions and developments and forward-policy thinking.

As a result, not many companies today have gutsy, timely management publications. Of the seventeen companies which contributed information used in this section of the book, only seven have the kind of publications which might fall into this category—and then only when evaluated under the most liberal of interpretations of purpose and content. Even after being established with lofty principles and hopes, some of these publications unfortunately fall victim to a variety of reasons (or excuses), including fears of disclosure of company secrets, too much candor for public view, and costs.

Here are reasons given by some of my associates for not having a top-caliber management publication:

- "Too cerebral."
- "Killed by management, who saw no value in it."
- "Its existence suggests a 'we-they' attitude."
- "We couldn't get enough new information for managers to make it worthwhile."

- "There were too many rungs in the approval ladder."
- "We can't get extra budget for it."
- "We had a good publication, but even moderate costs made it expendable."
- "We don't really believe in opening the company books."
- "It couldn't withstand the pressures of trying to make sense out of conflicting views of top-management executives on key issues."

Support for Management Publications. However, there is increasing support for the idea that a management publication can be a valuable communication channel—and particularly for multi-location organizations. Good management publications can be effective media not only for increasing the knowledge of managers and supervisors, but also for providing them with the ammunition they need to communicate better with the employees they supervise.

A management publication can serve many purposes. It should not be viewed as a news or news-interpretive magazine; most of the really big news matters will already have been covered by newspapers, radio and TV. But here are some of the most important potential benefits of a good management publication:

- As a unifying force in giving all managers a common basis for understanding company policies, business trends, issues and developments.

- To highlight examples of outstanding leadership styles and achievements, inside and outside the company.

- To promote fuller understanding of controversial issues by discussing both pros and cons. It can be an effective way to ensure that management's side of important issues is understood throughout the organization. This includes not only business subjects but also social-environmental-political issues that can have substantial effects on most institutions—public or private.

For maximum effectiveness, a management publication of this type should be published ten-to-twelve times a year at minimum.

To publish less frequently impairs continuity of messages and conveys an almost casual, "we'll-talk-to-you-once-in-a-while" attitude.

The publication doesn't have to be glossy and beautiful; in fact, these can be sources of criticism. But the publication should contain top-priority information, written well and honestly, and conveyed on a regular basis. Any company which can't meet these requirements shouldn't go through the trouble and expense of doing a management publication.

Decentralized Organizations. Those who operate in highly decentralized organizations raise a legitimate question in asking whether one management publication produced at central corporate headquarters can really do the job for every major unit. They point out that some divisions or groups have their own products, their own specific business goals, and in some respects, their own management styles. Why shouldn't they have their own management publications?

Maybe they should—but not necessarily at the expense of corporate publications. Employee communication managers wrestle constantly with the dilemma of how much is too much: When does repetition in robes of different organizational levels become unnecessary and costly redundancy?

Each company will have different answers to these questions, and the degree of centralization or decentralization will be an important consideration. If a second tier of management publications can serve meaningful purposes among their own management groups—such as increased understanding, ownership and ability to communicate with their employees—perhaps the potential payoff is worth the added investment.

However, it does seem that the more logical approach would be to incorporate in the corporate publication the kinds of materials which might have special appeal for the major divisions. In so doing, it would also enrich the content and breadth of the corporate publication for the benefit of all managers.

On the other hand, it is difficult to imagine divisional management publications communicating the quantity, tone and substance of corporate priorities and direction in the absence of a corporate magazine. No segment can speak for the whole corporate entity; this would be true of both employee and management publications.

Need for Broad-Based Corporate Support. Dick Madden, internal communications director at Allstate Insurance Company, says decentralized companies like his must also pay special attention to the need for broad-based communication to management people in many key areas of the business.

> While it is important that our major units have strong individual identities, there are critical issues facing our total business which require solid understanding and support from all our employees, and particularly our managers. This is crucial to employee performance and attitudes, but also necessary for employee understanding of the possible impact that new government regulations can have on our business and their own job security.

J&J Managers Fill Important Role. Johnson & Johnson's highly-decentralized management philosophy calls for no direct corporate communication with its more than 60,000 non-managerial employees around the world. J&J has 167 operational units in fifty-four countries. Also, according to Larry Foster, corporate vice president for public relations, it does not "dictate to individual managements that they show a video or distribute company publications to all managers or employees."

Johnson & Johnson looks to its 25-year-old *Worldwide* publication to fill an important role in keeping its 17,500 managers up-to-date—and through them, all employees. *Worldwide* is a four-color magazine published five times a year, and it is usually twenty pages in length.

The company's management communication program also includes a newsletter-type *Worldwide News Digest* (about every 3 weeks) and video network programs (ten times a year).

Foster says, "*Worldwide* is designed to communicate company philosophy, important business happenings and to give managers a feeling of belonging in a highly decentralized and geographically dispersed company."

The magazine discusses a wide range of subjects, including highlights of annual stockholder meetings and management conferences as well as management tips. Heavy coverage is given to new products and to discussions of health fields in which the company makes important contributions.

Controversial subjects are discussed, but the magazine doesn't "look for trouble." Some examples include:

- how the executive compensation plan rewards excellence in management,
- a healthy view of corporate contributions,
- lessons learned from the Tylenol tampering crisis, and
- the case for animal testing, which has made giant advances in medicine possible (examples: polio, cancer chemotherapy, and heart surgery and transplants).

AT&T's Ray O'Connell emphasizes the importance of the *AT&T Journal* which replaced three existing management publications after "the painful divestiture" of AT&T in 1984. He says the new publication was designed to be a unifying force, to develop an understanding of the direction and priorities of the total enterprise, and "to assure managers and employees that we're all on the same team and pulling together in the right direction."

If a management publication is really effective, its philosophy and editorial format will be as unique as that organization is, compared to others in the business world. The difference in approaches by General Motors, AT&T, Johnson & Johnson, Allstate and Chevron illustrates this point. (See Case Example 6 on the *AT&T Journal* at the end of this chapter, pages 104-7.)

The GM Journal. Introduction of *The Journal*—"A Magazine for General Motors Leadership"—in December 1985 was a bold thrust to open up previously restricted channels of communication to the company's total management group. It is a bimonthly, simple-format, sixteen to twenty page magazine which is distributed to the desks of managers and supervisors.

The magazine focuses on major internal and external issues affecting the company, the industry and the future, plus case examples of effective management styles or techniques both inside and outside of the company. It seeks to define the corporation mission and direction, while also reflecting the desires, hopes and concerns of the entire management organization, not just top company executives.

The Journal does not attempt to be a news magazine. Rather, it gives special attention to background and to the interpretations of events, plans or trends affecting the company's business. The magazine is also committed to exploring sensitive and controversial subjects of high interest and concern to managers and all employees. In fact, many management publications have failed because of restraints on what could be reported.

Management publications should be aggressive in reporting corporate strategy, thinking and reasons for decisions.

Andrea Koterba, manager of GM employee communications on the corporate public relations staff, says:

> To be most effective, a management publication should be as aggressive as possible in digging out and reporting corporate strategy, thinking and reasons for decisions. That's particularly true of the tough, unpopular actions like closing of plants or benefits modifications. If managers aren't in sync with what the corporation is doing and why, how can we expect them to explain or defend corporate positions to their people or to non-GM people?

Koterba says that after *The Journal's* introduction, the first couple of years involved a lot of hard selling on the advantages of a consistent, open-communication philosophy. And the publication slowly gained credibility in the way it handled previously untouchable subjects. Some examples:

- Why was GM closing 11 plants permanently?
- Why some component operations might close if they can't compete.
- What was the story behind executive bonuses when there was no profit sharing for employees? and,

- What were the reasons for GM's loss in market share in the 80s?

Koterba says *The Journal's* achievements in this respect have also led to broader coverage of sensitive areas in other corporate activities, particularly the monthly, all-employee tabloid, *GM Today*. In addition, high-level management has been very helpful.

> Advice and support from an editorial advisory board composed of nine top corporate executives has been of tremendous help in forging a more forthright, more expansive reporting of corporate matters.
>
> Having active participation and support at this level helps insulate the publication from a lot of arbitrary editing and political pressures, particularly at mid-management levels.

Management Videotapes

Videotapes are enjoying increasing popularity as a vehicle for communicating with managers and supervisors, and also as a tool which supervisors can use in conducting meetings with their own employees.

Videotapes offer several advantages over other media. Fast and flexible production, and electronic editing and availability of a variety of special effects make high quality and dramatic impact relatively easy to achieve. Playback capabilities are a real plus, particularly when videos are used for training purposes.

Highly important is the fact that videotapes, as is true with television generally, have high basic credibility with viewers. The American people are indeed infatuated with the TV screen and spoiled by the high-quality shows produced by the networks and also by major city news organizations. However, because employees are used to reasonably high-quality news productions on TV, they expect similar quality in company videotapes—and that requires expertise, time and money.

Videotapes can be an effective means of promoting more regular communication by providing basic information from corporate or divisional levels, information which can be used as a foundation for local activities. Leader training-guides increase the potential for lively, two-way discussion.

Johnson & Johnson produces about sixty videotapes a year for its 17,500-member management organization located at some 200 locations around the world. Subjects include stockholders' meetings, important company and industry news plus special programs on significant developments and strategic issues of the company's major business units.

Management Conference Videotapes. An important recent development at General Motors has been the distribution of videotaped highlights of previously "for-your-eyes-only" management conferences of 500 to 900 top executives.

A June 1986 management conference came at a very difficult time for GM, and a 66-minute videotape with conference highlights conveyed that message clearly. The videotape included an urgent appeal for improved quality and reduced costs. It discussed previously taboo subjects such as comparing the competition's labor costs for building vehicles, comparing the product quality ratings of the company's chief competitors, and the failure of operating units to meet projected budget reductions by a substantial amount.

The videotape also included a statement by GM President Jim McDonald, in which he told the group: "I don't really feel I can say I'm proud of you because we haven't accomplished what we set out to do in quality improvement and cost reduction."

It was a tough message that needed to be conveyed—not just to the 500 attendees, but to the entire management organization. More than 40,000 managers viewed the videotape. Most locations used it as part of 2-hour sessions, some involving salaried and hourly employees as well.

Viewers gave the videotape high marks for its lay-it-on-the-line approach. More than eighty-five percent said the videotape helped them to understand the company's serious challenges.

Preparation of videotaped highlights and accompanying digests of management conferences is now almost standard procedure at GM. Following management conferences for more than 900 top executives in Traverse City, Michigan, in 1988 and 1989, videotape and written highlights were made available to GM's top management group for use in preparing their own local communication packages for other managers and employees.

Security for such programs can be a serious problem—particularly when thousands of tapes are distributed to hundreds of locations, or if additional copies are made by local units from satellite copies. Actually, GM has had a minimum of leaks.

However, when a financial analyst told Chairman Roger Smith that he was very impressed with the June 1986 conference videotape—and that he had a copy—it rattled the dishes in the GM building in Detroit for quite a while.

Satellite Television

For an increasing number of organizations, satellite TV is the medium of the future for management communication. It provides a tremendous opportunity for top company executives to have regular meetings with field executives in live, interactive discussions on a variety of subjects.

Many companies are moving ahead to establish satellite capabilities covering both U.S. and overseas locations. Eleven of the sixteen companies that contributed information used in this section of the book use satellite TV for communicating with their management people, and four are also using it for communicating with all employees, as discussed more fully in Chapter VI.

Industry sources say that seventy private satellite networks are now operating in the U.S., and the number is still rising.

Nearly 10,000 Organizations Use TV. Douglas and Judith Brush, consultants who have chronicled private television growth in this country since 1974, say the number of U.S. organizations using TV has increased since that time from 300 to 9,500. In the 1988 D/J Brush study of 100 companies using television as a communication medium, employee information has replaced training as the most important video application, followed by sales training, skills training and product demonstrations.

Major opportunities exist for using satellite TV for such general communication activities as management conferences and press conferences. But the greatest potential appears to be for teleconferences in specialized areas such as marketing, personnel, manufacturing and engineering—and particularly in those industries whose special emphasis is on materials designed for dealer organizations. Its capability for two-way discussions by audio or video increases the potential of this medium significantly.

Allstate Uses TV for Management Communication. Allstate Insurance Company uses the Sears Satellite Network to televise quarterly top-level management conferences to its forty U.S. locations. About 800–1,000 managers attend Chicago sessions, and another 500 high-level executives see it on satellite TV at the company's forty field locations.

Subjects deal with a variety of information, including company philosophies, profit and loss projections, company goals, problems and major business and public issues. The telecast reports the entire conference—the average length is typically about three hours—including Q&A sessions. (Use of satellite TV by Ford Motor Company and Federal Express—including management programs—is covered in case examples at the end of Chapters 6 and 8, respectively.)

Advantages and Disadvantages of TV. Traditionalists say that personal dynamics and the warmth of face-to-face management meetings can't be matched by a teleconference—and they are right. Teleconferencing can never replace face-to-face gatherings. But it can supplement these meetings, allowing for an increased number of get-togethers at relatively modest additional cost.

Quarterly interactive TV programs, for example, would seem to be a logical way of keeping the management group up-to-date on corporate priorities. The Q&A portions of the televised sessions would also provide a channel for regular feedback about field management questions and concerns. The quarterly management forums would be particularly effective for multi-location organizations.

Also, for those companies with regular management videotape programs, satellite broadcasts can eliminate the costly, timely and burdensome distribution of tapes by mail to each location.

One of the biggest barriers to greater use of this medium for high-level management communication is the perceived inability to guarantee security. Once this fear is eliminated—and it can be—

satellite conferences will become an important medium of management communication. Increasing the skills of executives in how to use this medium and raising their confidence in its potential will help to expand its use. Potential savings in travel, housing and dining costs—plus the saved travel time of executives—add significantly to the attractiveness of satellite communication. Facilities also can be commercially rented for telecasts to most major cities in North America.

SUMMARY

Top managers in every organization must establish the policies, climate, incentives and the example of good communications necessary to carry out their leadership responsibilities. It is essential that formal communication activities be established for an on-going exchange of important business information with all managers using a variety of media.

Corporate policies, recommendations and service activities can only be as effective as their execution at the local levels. That's where communication is most meaningful in terms of work goals and job security.

In every organization, all managers and supervisors must accept the responsibility for communication—the sharing of information and ideas—if the process is to produce the greatest benefits. In turn, top management must provide problem-oriented communication training as well as promotion and incentive systems which recognize and reward good communicators.

In addition to the bottom-line use of communication to help improve work performance, honest and timely communication is also critical for understanding, trust and job satisfaction among all employees.

CASE 5

GM'S Delco Moraine-NDH Division

TOUGH EXPECTATIONS
OF A FRONT-LINE MANAGER
ABOUT THE ROLE
OF COMMUNICATION

We cannot be world class in our business unless we have world-class employee communication to support our business objectives, and truly effective communication definitely represent a competitive advantage.

These are the opinions of Glenn Reeser, who directs the bearings business unit of the Delco Moraine-NDH Division of General Motors. At 43, he has been with three divisions in twenty-two years with GM. His operation has 2,700 employees in Sandusky, Ohio, and Bristol, Connecticut, producing mainly front-wheel-drive bearings for GM motor vehicles.

Reeser is typical of a new breed of manager at GM—open, honest, strong on participative management, obsessed with being world class and beating all competition, both domestic and foreign. He views communication as a valuable resource in beating the competition—no easy assignment.

He expects the 1990s to be turbulent for the American auto industry and for American business in general.

Worldwide competition will become even more intense, fueled by the dramatic changes occurring in Europe especially.

There will be a great influx of investment capital into these countries, and out of North America. Sales and profit gains will be much tougher for American producers. As a result, the need for effective communication to achieve greater employee understanding and cooperation will be even more essential to our business success.

OVERALL CONCEPTS OF COMMUNICATION

Reeser is a strong believer in sharing virtually all business information with employees.

> About ninety-eight percent of every thing I know as unit director should be communicated to employees. We're all in it together; there are essentially no secrets. And because we have unions, I believe strongly that our communication program—like the work responsibilities—should be done jointly.

His current communication system relies heavily on face-to-face activities, including quarterly state-of-the-business conferences for the union and management leadership groups. Videotaped highlights of these sessions are produced for give-and-take meetings for remaining employees. Print activities include a daily newsletter, a monthly tabloid and an employee annual report. Closed-circuit TV is used for communicating simple, visual messages on a regular basis and for telecasting special events.

Reeser has very high expectations of his employee communicator. He expects the communicator to be bluntly frank in warning him of possibly wrong communication decisions and to push him into taking calculated risks when the situation requires. He places a high priority on continuous improvement and continuous feedback in adding value to the communication process.

What follows are Reeser's comments on three key elements in the relationship between manager and communicator:

1. What he expects from his communicator;
2. What the manager should do to empower his communicator so he or she can do an effective job; and
3. What are the biggest deficiencies he has observed in communicators?

Manager's Expectations of Communicator

1. *A professional with the right degree of professional wisdom in the communication area.* This requires not only communication training and experience, but equally important, a broad background in the business, its major elements and its people—and a natural skill in interrelating all of these elements to properly reflect the organization.
2. *One who maintains an active network throughout the organization.* This involves other professionals in the organization and also

regular contacts with a variety of people at all levels of the organization and community.

3. *A person with the ability to put together a sound communication plan.* The plan should provide overall direction around the organization's goals, but it must also show flexibility to respond to new circumstances. "A good plan may predict some twenty-five percent of actions required; the other seventy-five percent will be on-the-spot responses to new situations."

4. *A professional who knows the audience and environment.* He or she must know the basic needs and desires of employees and must also know how to deal with the politics of the organization.

5. *The ability to identify the most effective media for communicating certain types of information.* Among the options are face-to-face meetings, or written or visual materials.

6. *The ability to recognize and identify unusual opportunities for using communication.* Such opportunities can serve as a means of making events or plans more successful or to control the magnitude of damage in crisis situations.

7. *A communication plan characterized by continuous improvement.* This requires experimenting with new ideas and placing strong emphasis on feedback using both formal and informal methods of evaluation.

8. *A commitment to maintain the integrity of the communication system.* "Evasive or unclear messages can lead employees to believe that you are manipulating or even lying to them. Communicators must point out aggressively when planned management actions may be putting the integrity of the communication process in jeopardy."

9. *A communication system that doesn't speak down to employees.* "Employees are not children but smart, fully-functioning adults capable of understanding complex business issues and events going on in the world."

10. *A willingness to help other professionals in the organization become better communicators.* This also includes the need to educate the entire organization about the importance of communication in achieving individual and organizational goals.

Empowering the Communicator

1. *Providing access to virtually all business information.* This includes attendance at key staff meetings. "The organization needs to see the communicator as almost an 'independent third party,' one who has the total confidence of top management in doing what is right for employees as well as management in the communication process."

2. *Making the communicator's role clear to the entire organization.* This is particularly critical for staff and supervisory people. "The organization should know from the top about communication goals and how top management has empowered the communicator to do the job."

3. *Providing an efficient, minimum-clearance procedure.* This must be based on trust and confidence in the communicator to do the right thing and to seek multiple approvals only when required by unusual situations.

Deficiencies in Communicators' Performance

1. *Easily intimidated by people in positions of authority.* "There's a lot of intimidation in running a business; it's just a fact of life. Communicators must have the courage to challenge authority when it is standing in the way of effective communication."

2. *Sometimes easily frustrated.* "This is a problem when they lose a battle or can't convince management to do the right thing. On these occasions, communicators need to be even more aggressive; they must be more persistent when they know they're right."

3. *Becoming 100 percent absorbed with "happy talk."* "Some gossipy, social-type stories can be a 'hook' for enticing employees to read a publication, but they cannot be allowed to dominate the communication effort because there's too much hard, tough news about the business which employees need and deserve to know."

4. *Lacking strong planning abilities.* Communicators must know how to think out and organize both short- and long-range action plans.

5. *Failure to stay in touch with their environment.* Successful networking and spending time in all parts of the organization are critical for keeping close tabs on the pulse of the work environment and employees.

Reeser is critical of managers who do not provide "by-example" leadership to the communication function.

Executives in some organizations are even more guilty of neglect in maintaining personal relationships and understanding with the people they manage. Managers should spend less time behind their desks and more time among employees to stay abreast of their reactions, concerns and needs...

Some managers use the communication function (and public relations, too) as a dumping ground for people who couldn't do anything else well. That does a great disservice to the communication function and to the entire organization.

CASE 6

American Telephone & Telegraph Corporation

AFTER THE PAIN OF DIVESTITURE
AT&T JOURNAL WAS A STRONG
UNIFYING FORCE

When the *AT&T Journal* was created in late 1985, its target readers were first- and second-line managers with substantial responsibility. Typically, they were veterans of the pre-divestiture Bell System who were shell-shocked by an avalanche of change. According to Ray O'Connell, division manager of public relations:

> *AT&T Journal* emerged as a potentially powerful medium for unifying and assuring managers that indeed there was life after divestiture; of providing a clear vision of direction and confidence; and for helping managers reorient their thinking and responsibilities in the radically changed environment of the new AT&T.

MANAGERS ILL-PREPARED FOR DIVESTED ENVIRONMENT

Experience with the Bell System left most AT&T managers ill-prepared for the leap into a divested environment, O'Connell pointed out.

> Old loyalties and expectations fostered in a regulated monopoly environment clashed with the harsh realities of a fiercely competitive marketplace.
> A wave of downsizings—through layoffs and early retirement programs—trimmed the company's work force from about 375,000 at divestiture in 1984 to some 305,000 in 1989. This was painful for managers who had grown up in a working environment which promised lifetime employment security for themselves and their employees.

From a communication standpoint, there was a serious problem involving cohesiveness and unity in a very traumatic period. The corporation's major units—AT&T Communications, Information Systems, Network Systems, Bell Laboratories, and AT&T Technologies—had employee communication programs which operated independently in developing strong identities for their own units.

A small corporate staff worked to provide all AT&T managers with the information needed to understand broad, overall corporate priorities and direction. Among its efforts were reports on important corporate events and developments which were syndicated to all business units, a quarterly magazine for middle- and upper-level managers, and special events broadcast to managers via closed circuit TV.

But the primary responsibility for employee communication was decentralized, resting firmly in the hands of employee communication managers in the business units. Their priorities were to support the objectives and employee information needs of their own organizations.

This policy had serious limitations from the corporate viewpoint. It gave managers and employees a narrow view since there was no vehicle to develop understanding of the direction and priorities of the total enterprise.

"SINGLE-ENTERPRISE" STRATEGY

Top management called for a "single-enterprise strategy"—declaring that AT&T could not operate successfully as a holding company running disconnected businesses. All business units work from a common technology base, market a common brand and profit from the reputation of the total company. Also, there is a strong interdependence among business units, with sophisticated projects often requiring contributions from several units.

O'Connell said that this placed a premium on cooperation rather than inter-unit competition—leading to a broader base of common understanding and shared values among company managers.

A more efficient employee information system was also needed to support common values and understanding among åll employees. A top-level task force composed of executives from major business units recommended the consolidation of key employee communication functions at the corporate level.

A key proposal was for a new monthly publication for all managers, replacing three existing AT&T publications distributed to various groups of managers. A bimonthly publication—Focus—is mailed to the homes of all 300,000 AT&T employees. Coordination of all TV work also was consolidated at corporate level.

HEAVY BUSINESS ORIENTATION

The *AT&T Journal* is a three-color monthly magazine, typically running sixteen-to-twenty pages and distributed to about 100,000 managers at work. It is not designed as a news or news-analysis publication, but it is heavily oriented toward the business. Its main objectives are:

- To help supervisors carry out AT&T strategy.
- To help them better understand the work environment.
- To help supervisors in their efforts to encourage positive behaviors in their employees, such as teamwork, bottom-line orientation, customer focus, attention to quality and cost, and management of change.
- To help managers and employees understand the linkages between the company's priorities and their own jobs.

SUPPORTS SUPERVISOR AS PRIMARY COMMUNICATOR

As O'Connell said,

> the publication is designed to support the individual supervisor in the role of primary communicator for the company. Supervisors are encouraged to share information in *AT&T Journal* with their employees through face-to-face discussions or by passing around their copies of the magazine.

In addition to executive interviews on the state-of-the business, here are other articles which illustrate the mission of *AT&T Journal*:

- *"The Renaissance Manager."* This feature highlighted operating styles which the company leaders expect from managers—stressing a stronger focus on unleashing the creativity of employees, greater decision-making authority and accountability, and on-going performance feedback. As the article headlined: "The role of leaders has shifted from boss to champion."
- *"Managing in the 1990s: Versatility, Flexibility and a Wide Range of Skills."* This story examined the results of a study of management skills required for success in the next decade.
- *"The New American Work force."* This article reviewed the nation's rapidly shifting demographics and the implications for both employers, managers and employees.
- *"Playing It Safe May be Risky Business."* The theme of this story was: "Failure is viewed as an opportunity for learning, not punishing."

O'Connell said:

> The *AT&T Journal* provides a window of understanding on the direction of the business and the expectations of top management—both

for AT&T and the company's major units. Following the painful divestiture, the magazine has been a strong unifying force, helping to assure managers and employees that we're all on the same team and pulling together in the right direction.

AT&T JOURNAL MOVES TO "HIGHER CAUSE"

After four years of very successful publication, the AT&T Journal ceased publication at the end of 1989 and its spirit moved on to a "higher cause."

The magazine had done exceptionally well in promoting unity and corporate purpose in the management group following the divestiture. But its success in bringing more corporate strategy information to the management group raised questions about why all employees should not receive such information directly.

After careful consideration, the decision was made to incorporate the basic goals and content priorities of AT&T Journal into the corporation's employee publication Focus, which is mailed to employee homes. This broadened the target audience for these types of materials from 100,000 to about 300,000 AT&T employees, and at reduced costs.

As O'Connell said:

By bringing this strategic information to everyone, AT&T acknowledged that all employees, at every level of the business, have an important contribution to make to our success—and that they require this kind of high-level information to focus their efforts effectively.

Special communication materials will still be distributed to the management group whenever necessary, largely via electronic bulletins and TV broadcasts—and there will be supervisory discussion packages for special topics.

AT&T's experience dramatizes the question that many top executives ask when evaluating proposed separate management publications: "Is this extra expense really necessary?" If top management can honestly and aggressively elevate the level of business information they provide to the entire employee group, then the question of separate management publications for many organizations may indeed be moot.

But are most managements today ready to make that kind of commitment for broad employee distribution of company information traditionally regarded as "confidential"?

Chapter 5

Research: Indispensable Tool: For Proving the Value of Communication

One of the most frustrating aspects of employee communication is knowing you're making a significant contribution to organizational goals—but you can't produce hard data to prove it.

It's a serious dilemma for professional communicators—whether they're employed by profit or nonprofit organizations, public or private. Non-profit organizations also have a bottom-line; it's just measured a little differently. In fact, generally speaking, dollars are tighter and value justification tougher for non-profits.

Every professional communicator worth his or her salt tries to prove the value of the efforts he or she directs. And there are a lot of ways to probe the elusive question: "How am I doing?" Recent advances in communication research technology show encouraging promise and also some fundamental deficiencies which need special attention.

VARIETY OF FORMAL AND INFORMAL METHODS

Informal samplings can provide some evidence of how employees feel about communication efforts.

Walk around the plant or offices and ask people what they think, what changes they'd like to make, whether they believe what they read or see or hear. Focus-group discussions can be helpful, but results can be overly negative and must be weighted accordingly. Readership surveys can provide useful information if the survey form is brief, the questions simple and clear, and you get a reasonable percentage of returns. Most experts believe that fifteen to twenty-five percent will produce reasonably solid data.

The biggest fault with informal samplings is that they have little or no scientific validity, and they are tough to sell to hard-nosed managers. But they do provide some valuable insights into employee opinions and should be a regular part of the on-going communication activity.

Because these types of informal research methods are inexpensive, they are an important resource for internal communicators in all types of organizations. But make use of professional associates familiar with testing technology and procedures (or outside consultants) to find the best way to carry out these evaluation forays.

Telephone surveys also can provide useful information if the survey is fairly simple and the interview is brief—10 minutes would be ideal. Telephone surveys should be conducted only by professional researchers. The main drawbacks of telephone research are intrusion on employees' personal time, distractions at home or work, and variations in personnel conducting the interviews.

What's a healthy approach to research?

Use a regular schedule of informal methods to give you running checks for mid-course corrections. The more scientific they can be, the better.

COMPREHENSIVE COMMUNICATION AUDIT

But also try to use comprehensive communication audits as a regular part of your evaluation schedule. They can provide much more valuable information, yielding results which are more acceptable to executives who have been bred on the value of scientific analysis of problems and possible solutions.

Having them done by outside consultants is highly desirable from the standpoints of both general expertise and credibility for management. But lack of funds for outside consultants should not be used as a reason (or excuse) for not doing comprehensive audits, particularly if in-house experts in behavioral psychology and survey skills are available.

While there are many ways of organizing a comprehensive audit, the most complete format would involve four parts:

1. One-on-one interviews with top executives,

2. Focus-group discussions,

3. A well-conceived survey questionnaire, which benefitted from the interviews and focus discussions and which is administered in sit-down meetings to representative groups of employees, or, in smaller organizations, to all employees, and

4. A critical analysis of the strategic communication plan, how the function is organized and the variety and quality of media used.

The most effective total diagnostic systems are ones which use follow-up research in the intervals between full-blown audits. This should be done each year if possible and can be done mostly with informal methods. This is important for monitoring improvements introduced into the system as a result of the audits; these follow-ups also show how the improvements are perceived by employees. Focus-group sessions are an appropriate method for these follow-up checks, the addition of interviews with key executives enhances the value and credibility of the studies.

Sometimes a combination of executive interviews and focus-group discussions allows an organization to evaluate the communication system faster and at less cost than the comprehensive four-phase audit. Disadvantages of this two-phase technique are that the results tend to have a shotgun rather than a rifle pattern, since they are skewed to negative aspects and provide no quantitative data so essential for selling results to managers. (See how Weyerhaeuser Paper Company used the executive interviews and focus-group combination in Case Example 7 at the end of this chapter on pages 124-26.)

Skilled conduct of both the interviews and discussion sessions can keep the main focus on priority areas and keep positive-negative extremes to a minimum. A mini-questionnaire of twenty to twenty-five questions at the end of focus group discussions is a simple and effective way of adding hard data.

Time Span Is Critical Factor

The biggest disadvantages of the four-phase communication audits are the cost and time involved from the beginning of preliminary discussions to completion of the final report, which includes recommended improvement actions. Obviously, both are serious obstacles.

In fact, the critical nature of the time lapse is often not given proper attention. The result is stale data and diminished enthusiasm, particularly in the participating organizations. Rigid target dates should be established for each phase of the study—whether done internally or externally.

First Audits Need Special Care

In the case of first audits, particularly when outside consultants are used, the study should examine the structure of the communication function, its strategic plan, the variety of media and the quality of materials being used in carrying out the communication program.

Are there both long- and short-term plans? How are they developed? How often? What media are used and how? How is the employee communication function organized at the company level? How are company-wide efforts coordinated? What type of in-house or outside research is done to test effectiveness? The question of sufficient staff and budget should also be raised.

These are key questions which should be given serious consideration in the total audit study and report. In these basic areas, particularly, outside consultants can be of great help to in-house communication specialists because of their breadth of knowledge gained through work with other companies.

Executive Reports Should Be Clear, Concise

The communication manager should insist that the final report for executives—including recommendations—be clear, concise and not more than 30-minutes in length, but additional data should be available on request. Most executives are looking for a simple evaluation report and conclusions, plus a handful of recommendations on how to improve the system. They don't want to have to be led through an encyclopedia of data to get to the bottom line.

DEVELOPING A SURVEY QUESTIONNAIRE

In developing a survey questionnaire, here are several suggestions:

- Make sure you select the right executives for interviews, at various levels and in important related areas such as human resources. These are key people who can provide good input and on-going support for your total communication program.
- Seek advice from organizational research and development professionals within the company in developing the questionnaire. Outside counselors cannot be expected to know about in-house pitfalls, politics and other sensitivities that could produce distorted responses or criticism by management or unions.
- Keep the questions brief and clear, and keep the questionnaire as short as possible, requiring no more than one hour of time involvement by participating employees.
- Advise the unions of plans, and let them know how unionized employees will be involved. Let them see the questionnaire before it is final, and ask for their cooperation in the project.

Surveys Provide Variety of Information

Scientific surveys can provide a variety of information on many subjects, such as:

- What do employees feel about the overall effectiveness of communication?
- How do their perceptions compare with previous years?
- Where do employees get their business information?
- What sources are most believable?
- How do they rate their supervisors on two-way communication practices?

A questionnaire survey can provide valuable information in other areas. How well do employees believe the company communicates on specific subjects like benefit changes, acquisitions or mergers, and major organizational changes? How well informed do employees think they are on subjects critical to the success of the business? How many employees actually read, understand and believe employee publications?

And don't forget to include an open-ended question or two at the end so employees can express in their own words what they think about communication where they work—and offer ideas for improvement. The structured questions provide quantitative data— and that's certainly essential—but open-ended questions provide expressions from the heart that warm and personalize the hard facts that the rest of the questionnaire produces.

Excellent Upward Communication Medium

The survey also is an excellent avenue for upward communication. And open-ended questions provide employees with a welcome window for talking to management. Most employees take advantage of this window—some in strong, critical language. Reading, categorizing and summarizing these comments for management takes a great deal of time. But it's worth every minute invested—for both executives and communication people.

And for heaven's sake, tell the manager the whole truth from the survey results: no rose without the thorns.

Ignoring or hiding the bad news in a survey—even if some of the comments get a little personal—does a serious disservice to the CEO or to other executives at whatever level. Such shielding is patently dishonest and highly injurious to the credibility of the communication effort—and of management, too.

But shielding the identity of employee respondents to a questionnaire or discussion session should be viewed as a sacred trust. Obviously, the greatest value of surveys comes from honest, candid perceptions of employees, even if the perceptions are incorrect.

Human nature being what it is, there are some bosses, even in the most progressive companies, who would object strenuously to criticism by employees and would seek their own form of retribution. In the least progressive companies, where the need for constructive criticism is the greatest, anonymity for employee comments is also the most critical.

MANAGERS' VIEW OF RESEARCH

How do today's managers view communication surveys/audits? In my experience, very favorably, particularly if they are part of a well-developed plan with management input and with the clear objective of making improvements.

It is naive to expect managers to buy a "pig in a poke." Magic words and dazzling visuals may be impressive in communication products. It is a field which unfortunately is susceptible to fads like Information Racks, electronic bulletin boards and, occasionally still, free turkeys which are offered in contests to improve some phase of employee performance.

But more and more, if professionals can't prove that employee communication activities are earning their keep, they may be in serious jeopardy—and rightfully so.

Mike Emanuel, writing in *Inside Organizational Communication,* said:

> Senior management is far more involved in communication than ever before, and communicators and their programs are being scrutinized far more critically because they are being seen as essential contributors to profit-and-loss statements. This is the reason why there is widespread interest in the communication audit. It makes good business sense and takes its place alongside other organizational reviews: the financial audit, the benefits review, strategic planning, market research and manpower-needs analysis.[1]

Feedback Commitment Is Important

Before planning a survey, get a definite commitment from management that highlight results will be fed back to all supervision and employees, along with a report of actions being taken to correct deficiencies.

Under ideal circumstances, presentations should be made to the local management group at facilities participating in the study. These presentations should discuss local results—compared with division and/or corporate findings—and also recommendations for improvements. Top local management should participate in these

---

[1] Myron Emanuel, "Auditing Communication Practices," from INSIDE ORGANIZATIONAL COMMUNICATION, edited by Carol Reuss and Donn Silvis, p. 46. Copyright (c) 1985 by Longman Publishing Group. Reprinted by permission of Longman Publishing Group.

presentations—at least the action part—to send a clear message of participation in and support of proposed-improvement efforts.

It is important that highlight results also be provided for the entire employee group—with the employee publication being an ideal channel.

If the organization doesn't report both highlight results and action plans to employees, the survey process can boomerang. When employees take the time to offer suggestions about improving communication performance at their location and hear nothing about the results or actions being taken by management, they are disappointed, and management credibility takes a nose dive. In addition, much of the long-range potential of the survey, in terms of employee expectations and confidence, will be lost.

Scientific research, using the latest technology, can convince most managers that effective communication can make a significant contribution to the business and can give solid guidance for improvements. The comprehensive audit has been the mainstay for this type of research over the last decade or so.

EVALUATION SHOULD PERMEATE COMMUNICATION PROCESS

But the evaluation process is most effective when it permeates the entire communication process every day. Test and audit essentially everything—on a running basis. Major long-range activities should be evaluated from time-to-time to allow for running changes. Focus group discussions are good for on-going activities.

Where possible, subject new projects to pre-launch pilot tests, with participants giving ratings and criticisms. Some examples include communication training or new publications for managers.

Get the meanest, most critical people to give you honest ideas for improving a project — or trashing it.

The idea is to get the meanest, most critical people you know to give you honest ideas for improving a project—or for trashing it.

Tough managers are the most desirable "test pilots." They know that time spent in training must be earned back in improved performance on either a short- or long-term basis.

A new management publication has to be meaningful in terms of upgrading the performance of supervisors and in very pragmatic terms. If you are on the right track, endorsement by these types of managers will provide powerful credibility—especially with other members of the management group, right up to the top.

For regular publications and management videotapes, consider the issue-by-issue evaluation system; this involves mailing brief survey cards to a sizable number of employees a week or two after each issue. These cards ask employees how well they recall certain types of articles; and they ask for a simple evaluation of key elements, along with ideas for improvement. This provides ammunition for continuous improvement, rather than having to make drastic improvements when formal surveys are done every 2 or 3 years.

Another idea is to fax copies of a survey form to representative employees on the job. This puts a more personalized request for help in the employee's hands, where it can be done as part of the work-day labor—rather than as homework which intrudes on personal time at home.

Never Be Afraid to Test New Ideas

Communicators should never be afraid to test good ideas. Results will add strength in content and overall relevance to on-the-job situations. They will also give the project a solid base of support in the entire management group—and among employees, too. Even if the idea's no good and is cancelled because of bad reviews, the communication manager shouldn't despair. The organization will save a lot of money, and the communication manager will avoid a lot of headaches and possible loss of credibility.

Professional communicators at most companies should be able to evaluate their own activities—even the comprehensive audit—using inside experts to obtain scientifically valid data that management will believe. The final analysis of data, conclusions and recommendations should be made by the company's employee communication manager. But hiring an outside consultant to assist in these phases could bring additional expertise and a third-party perspective both to the study findings and to the translation of results into an action plan.

Communication audits conducted for GM in 1982, 1984 and 1986 by Mike Emanuel had an important impact on the form and substance of GM's corporate-wide program; they also led to a higher level of management respect.

How often should comprehensive audits be done? At least every three years is desirable. This provides enough time for changes to take place and have an effect throughout the organization. It also is frequent enough to be a constant reminder for management that somebody is not only working hard at the communication job but is also keeping score. The three-year cycle is especially appropriate for companies which renegotiate labor contracts triennially.

USING AUDITS TO ADVANCE THE TOTAL SYSTEM

From the standpoint of managing and merchandizing the communication system, regular audits can provide:

- A systematic way of tracking performance and of reporting progress, or lack of it, to management.

- An evaluation of deficiencies and directions for making improvements.

- Direct involvement in the communication process by top management at corporate, divisional and plant levels—as well as by thousands of employees. Most employees love to be asked to participate in a survey; they're glad somebody wants their ideas.

- A method for making regular reports to both management and employees—not only through written reports and presentations, but also through management and employee publications and visual materials. This helps to foster a receptive, expectant environment for the total communication effort.

- An opportunity to demonstrate the value of the communication function to employees and managers at all levels of the organization, many of whom participate directly in various aspects of the studies.

RESEARCH RESULTS FROM SEVENTEEN-COMPANY COMPOSITE

Some of the most fundamental, continuing research in organizational communication has been conducted by Towers, Perrin, Forster and Crosby. Composite findings of studies in a variety of organizations have been published periodically since 1980 by TPF&C in cooperation with the IABC (International Association of Business Communicators) Research Foundation.

The latest report covers the 1987–89 period and includes 14,250 employees surveyed from seventeen companies in the U.S. and Canada.[2]

Steve Goldfarb, director of employee surveys for TPF&C, says the research shows that "employees are significantly better informed today, that communication is more complete, more direct, more honest and more relevant. Yet, employees are dissatisfied on many levels, with special desires for more face-to-face, two-way information-sharing from all levels of management, particularly senior executives."

Here are highlights of these studies as outlined by Goldfarb—a mixture of good news and bad news:

1. About three-fourths of the employees say their organization tries to keep them well informed about the business; this figure is relatively unchanged from previous studies.

2. Sixty-two percent of employees list top executives as a preferred source of information, but only fifteen percent say they actually get their company news from this source. Also, forty percent of employees surveyed don't think their management executives clearly explain the organization's goals—or how employees can contribute to the achievement of these goals.

[2] Julie Foehrenbach and Steve Goldfarb, "Employee Communication in the 90s: Great(er) Expectations," a joint report by the International Association of Business Communicators and Towers, Perrin, Forster & Crosby, April 1990.

3. Seventy-one percent of employees believe that communication from management is candid and accurate—up significantly from fifty-four percent in 1980. However, fifty-seven percent of employees say official communication activities do not tell the full story and only about half believe management and supervisors are good listeners.

4. Supervisors are doing a better job of communicating with their employees, and also are better informed by higher management, but employees express the desire for significant improvement in information-sharing with their supervisors.

5. The popularity and credibility of employee publications continue to rank very high—in the 90 percent range for readability and believability. However, only thirty-six percent prefer publications as a primary source of information.

6. Face-to-face communication is—and probably always will be—the preferred source of information for all employees, including managers, Goldfarb says.

These studies seem to indicate clear progress in organizational communication across the board. But hardly enough is being done to stay abreast of increasing demands by employees and management for higher and higher levels of two-way information sharing throughout their organizations.

COMMUNICATION TIES TO EMPLOYEE COMMITMENT

TPF&C research also shows that communication has a direct relationship to employee commitment. In turn, Goldfarb says: "High employee commitment has a favorable influence on key management goals, such as good service, productivity, low turnover of good workers, low absenteeism, employee activities as company ambassadors and favorable bottom-line results."

Goldfarb says: "The gist of this research is:

•   Commitment has been shown to have bottom-line implications in important areas such as "going the extra mile" or, on the other hand, such as we've seen in recent employee/management conflicts.

Commitment depends on confidence in leadership in such areas as management ability and efforts, rewards systems, training, collaborative behavior (empowerment), providing a free and open work environment and solid two-way communication to keep employees informed of how its management is carrying out its leadership responsibilities."

General Electric and Hewlett-Packard, in separate research efforts, have produced parallel results showing the relationship of supervisor communication to employee attitudes and bottom-line results. (See Case Example 8 at the end of this chapter, pages 127-28.)

The IABC-TPF&C survey reports and increased use of research by individual organizations certainly represent useful contributions toward a stronger scientific base for organizational communication.

RESEARCH DEFICIENCIES

But the scope and depth of research in this field is still inadequate. This is particularly true in terms of results which have day-to-day application for working professionals—and also in helping to prove the value of communication in achieving bottom-line results.

In fact, Joe Cahalan, director of corporate communications at Xerox, believes that lack of adequate research is a serious problem for the profession.

> We don't really know what works and why. As a whole, I think the profession shies away from research. We may actually be afraid to find out that some of our sacred cows are not really very effective. If we did more focused research, we would be more effective, have more clout and be more respected within our own organizations.

Traditional research, in my opinion, deals too much with recording past accomplishments or shortcomings and not enough with providing direction for future improvements. Professional researchers are often mesmerized by mountains of demographic computer printouts while giving short shrift to more fundamental questions and answers about "why" communication results happen and "how" to improve the system.

To be more effective, communication studies should probe such sensitive areas as employee awareness and comprehension of company missions and major problem areas, including those relating to both management and unions. They should seek to define basic human values in relation to the work environment and organizational goals—i.e., they should determine the trigger points for motivating employees to higher levels of performance and commitment—so that these can be incorporated into basic communication plans.

Need More Sophisticated Tools and Thinking

By and large, professional research is only scraping the skin, not cutting through to the bone of some of the critical needs of organizational communication. We need to develop more sophisticated tools and thinking.

Our profession needs to sell the value of scientific research more aggressively and to use it more regularly as a part of our professional approach to the communication task. Equally important, we must convince top management that regular research is an essential tool of evaluation and accountability—and also that prompt actions must be taken once research has spotlighted deficiencies and new directions.

A giant share of responsibility for upgrading the technology and acceptability of scientific research in this field falls on the shoulders of the leading professional organizations—in particular, this means the International Association of Business Communicators and the Public Relations Society of America.

But colleges and universities also have an important role to play. They are essential instruments not only for advancing research technology, but also in stressing to future practitioners its importance—and in stressing how to use it productively.

It is most important that mainline research done by, or in cooperation with, universities be directed to practical front-line problems. And the results should be translated in understandable language which can serve both practitioners and scholars.

Certainly, there is a place for theory and scholarly exchange of information. But providing valuable new data for stimulating or supporting productive actions in all kinds of organizations should be the essential goal, particularly for business and professional research projects.

SIX-YEAR STUDY BY IABC RESEARCH FOUNDATION

The six-year research project by the IABC Research Foundation, entitled *Excellence in Public Relations and Communication Management,* is a highly commendable activity in this direction. A total of 300 representative companies in North America and the United Kingdom will participate. Directed by Dr. James Grunig of the University of Maryland College of Journalism, the study is scheduled for completion in 1992.

The project is designed to probe key areas such as the common elements of excellent communication programs, how good communication can help organizations function more effectively and how much an excellent communication program is actually worth to an organization.

Professional communicators seek to relate their efforts in some way to bottom-line results—i.e., to helping the organization achieve more. This could be in terms of higher productivity or quality or better services—or in the case of most private organizations, to make more profit. But it is equally important to know the impact of communication efforts in reducing expenses. Some examples include avoiding conflicts or boycotts by constituencies or preventing enactment of unfair legislation—all of which could be expensive and have very negative effects on organizational results.

The IABC study will seek to develop ways of measuring how communication can and does affect both kinds of bottom-line performance. Much of the thrust of this study, in fact, is aimed at gutsy, practical aspects of communication, particularly communication as a critical management resource in today's highly competitive environment. It is a study long overdue.

As Maria Fort, executive director of the IABC Research Foundation says:

> Research has the potential for turning our profession from an art to at least a quasi-science endeavor, and that will make it much more acceptable in the boardrooms of American business. We hope this IABC study will be a big step toward that goal.

SUMMARY

Regular evaluation of employee communication activities is absolutely essential if they are to prove their value and provide the basis for continuous improvement. Both informal and formal techniques should be used, and the more scientific, the better. For maximum credibility and effectiveness, professional evaluations—including comprehensive audits—should be as regular as financial and quality audits.

Comprehensive audits every 3 years can give the employee communication program a solid basis for determining value and priorities, and it can do so in a professional manner that enhances the credibility of the system. Testing of specific activities—such as skills training, videotapes and new publications—before and after the fact also should be done on a continuing basis. Many organizations have in-house capabilities that can be used for these research activities.

Outside consultants can provide a broader perspective—plus analysis and action plans—that may be more objective and usually will have more credibility with top management than those of in-house experts.

Considerable work needs to be done in improving research technology in both context and scope, and in selling its importance as a fundamental tool of planning, evaluation and accountability.

```
CASE  7
Weyerhaeuser Paper Company
```

RESEARCH EMPHASIZES IMPORTANCE OF LOCAL COMMUNICATION

An excellent example of the use of the executive interview/focus-group combination for a comprehensive audit was carried out by Roger D'Aprix and Madeline Olson of TPF&C, for the Weyerhaeuser Paper Company, a part of the Weyerhaeuser Company which is headquartered near Tacoma, Washington. The paper company, which produces pulp, paper and packaging products, has 13,000 employees in some 100 U.S. operations.

PRODUCT QUALITY WAS MAJOR FOCUS

The purpose of the 1987 study was to evaluate the existing employee communication system—with a special emphasis on employee perceptions of product quality. The plan called for the results to be used to strengthen employee communication programs at company and local levels.

The project team interviewed thirty-one executives and led seventy-two focus-group discussions—including 800 employees at twenty-six company locations. It took nine weeks to do the research and another 6 weeks to gather and analyze the findings, according to Dan Koger, director of employee communications for Weyerhaeuser Paper at the time.

Koger said the executive interview/focus-group discussion approach provided the opportunity:

- To probe more fully the strengths and weaknesses of communication at each location,
- To get to know local management at one-fourth of the company's U.S. facilities and to introduce them to the concept of a planned communication system aimed at bottom-line results, particularly in the quality area,

- To give immediate feedback to local managers about what their employees felt; this contrasted with the long delays which result when questionnaires are the main source of information,
- To establish with local managers at this large number of facilities a direct involvement and ownership, not only in the current study but also in the development of a company-wide system of internal communication.

The Weyerhaeuser results were divided into three types of reports—a composite company report, five divisional reports and twenty-one reports covering each of the mills and plants that participated. This provided a broad foundation of information for use throughout the organization.

RESULTS CHANGED COMMUNICATION FOCUS

D'Aprix says the study stressed the need for consistent messages and the importance of local communication.

This audit—like so many others done for companies struggling to implement quality improvement—showed that people believed they were being rewarded not for quality but for volume of production. The communication system was sending one message, but the reward system was sending another—resulting in mixed signals and confusion about actual management goals.

The audit also confirmed the fact that employees felt their strongest allegiance to the location where they were employed. Divisional identities were abstractions for most of them, although there was a clear sense of pride in being associated with Weyerhaeuser. This finding led executives to focus communication efforts through local management, where they believed it would have the greatest impact.

FOLLOW-UP VISITS TO EACH LOCATION

On completion of the audit, company-wide results were presented to and discussed with top corporate executives, along with recommended improvements in the company's communication system. Follow-up visits were made by Koger to each participating division and plant location, where he discussed each unit's results in comparison with divisional and company results. These visits also provided the opportunity to work with local management in developing plans for making the improvements suggested by the study.

Koger stressed the importance of local unit managers in helping the company build a strong and durable employee communication program, and he emphasized the need for consultants to be creative in helping managers become better communicators.

Those front-line managers can make it or break it for a company. However, consulting is not a bunch of glamor trips but real pick-and-shovel work. A communicator has to be creative in tailoring solutions to each plant manager's own situation, and not be discouraged by rebuffs but be very persistent. Always try to come away with at least one improvement, regardless of how small; and build future efforts on this beachhead.

Eventually, the time will come when the pressure's on, the competition is beating at the door and the manager needs to get his people cranked up. That's when the basic principles, all the selling you've been doing, will begin to surface and you've got a manager/believer. In multi-plant companies, the one-on-one selling of top field managers is an important part of building a solid and durable system of communication.

Koger calls the audit findings a "living educational document, something concrete to have in your hands when you see plant or mill managers." He has used the survey results extensively in consulting activities with local units—not only with participants in the study but also at some of the company's seventy or so other U.S. operations as well.

PERSISTENCE AND CREATIVITY ARE KEYS

Koger says the audit played a key role in enabling substantial progress to be made in Weyerhaeuser communication during the several years following the study. Starting "almost from scratch," he said the survey results became an impressive tool for consulting activities.

In consulting with managers, we were able to present four or five basics of communication made apparent by the study. These are basics that almost everybody agrees should be done—such as a policy statement, getting all managers to assume responsibility for communication, the best media and the right business subjects. After that, however, the communicator must be creative and have a lot of persistence in his efforts to "get the managers into the communication game."

Managers want game plans that fit their specific problems, and they feel much more comfortable when they can have a big say in what they are. The communicator's job is to lay out the basics and then let the manager tailor-make his own formula and substance, with the communicator helping as much as possible.

```
CASE 8
General Electric and Hewlett-Packard Companies
```

RESEARCH TIES COMMUNICATION
TO EMPLOYEE COMMITMENT

Surveys at two major corporations—Hewlett-Packard and General Electric—have reinforced evidence that the better the manager communicates with his or her people on a face-to-face basis, the more satisfied employees are with their work life. And most experts agree that satisfied employees are more productive employees.

Until recently, few communicators had attempted to measure the effectiveness of managers' face-to-face communication skills or how they compared with respect to the mass media communication channels. According to Brad Whitworth, manager of employee communications for Hewlett-Packard Company, even fewer had tried to tie communication effectiveness to the possible contributions to bottom-line results of organizations.

COMMUNICATION HELPS JOB SATISFACTION

In the early 1980s, General Electric discovered a strong link between a manager's communication effectiveness and an employee's satisfaction on the job. In surveys involving thousands of employees, GE researchers discovered five survey questions that were a better predictor of an employee's overall satisfaction than any other question or group of questions. These had to do with how the employee's immediate supervisor handled job performance feedback, complaints, appraisals, compensation and career objectives in face-to-face discussions with his or her employees.

Hewlett-Packard, in analyzing its own questions from a 1985 survey, found five questions covering similar areas of face-to-face communication. These dealt with performance feedback, appraisals, help on the job, accessibility and overall performance in one-on-one meetings.

When asked how they would prefer to get company information, H-P employees in the 1985 survey ranked immediate managers at the top (93%), followed by interoffice memo (75%), local publications (75%) and other internal sources (43-65%). External media and grapevine ranked below twenty percent. The H-P results closely matched those secured earlier at GE, according to Whitworth. In both cases, employees who responded positively to these sets of five questions followed a similar pattern in answering other questions relating to their perception of their company, to their work environment and to how they were treated as employees.

At Hewlett-Packard, these responses included ones about how they perceived their work organization, its operating efficiency and management, their working relationships, communication, pay and benefits, working conditions, job satisfaction, performance and development, training, job security, company policies and practices and company image.

The conclusion: The better the manager communicates, the more satisfied the employees are with all aspects of their work life. Most managers at H-P, when shown these results, agreed that a more satisfied employee is a more productive employee.

INCREASED FOCUS ON MANAGERS

As a result, both GE and H-P have shifted the focus of much of their efforts to the immediate manager as the key link in the communication chain.

Whitworth, who served as chairman of the International Association of Business Communicators for the 1989–90 year, said that H-P is targeting more information directly to managers, and it's encouraging them to share it with their employees. The company is also putting more effort into training managers in communication skills.

In today's competitive environment, communicators who can quantitatively demonstrate their effectiveness are likely to see their employee communication programs fare well in the years ahead. And these results have convinced me—and many of the managers at H-P—that the bottom line of these studies is that organizations that are able to implement effective face-to-face communication programs at the employee level will have a competitive advantage in the future.

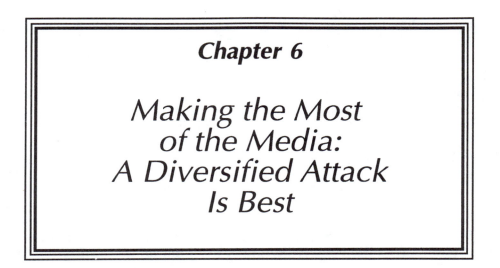

Chapter 6

Making the Most of the Media: A Diversified Attack Is Best

The most effective communication systems use a variety of communication channels to reach the total employee group.

The most fundamental and most important medium is face-to-face communication—one-on-one or in groups. Its greatest strengths come from the personal interactions between manager and employee—in the fact that employees are usually able to ask questions and get immediate answers—and as a result of the personal warmth and credibility it has compared with formal communication channels. Face-to-face communication is particularly important for sharing information that relates to job security or personal crises where the opportunity for two-way discussion is essential.

WIDE VARIETY OF CHANNELS IS AVAILABLE

But to be truly effective on an on-going basis in most organizations, face-to-face exchange of information should be supplemented by one or more additional formal media, such as telephones or electronic newslines, printed materials, videotape/film productions, closed-circuit (CCTV) or satellite television.

The external news media, although obviously less controllable and with less personal appeal than in-house activities, should also be considered when mapping total strategy. So should the grape-vine, usually "faster than a speeding bullet."

These are the major communication media, but there is a wide variety of other channels available—depending on how imaginative and how experimental the communicator wants to be in trying to find maximum exposure methods. Included are bulletin boards, booklets, payroll inserts, electronic bulletin boards, radio, executive letters to employee homes and executive speeches to employees in field plant or office locations.

Federal Express, Allstate Insurance Programs

Tom Martin, who directs employee communications at Federal Express, is a strong advocate of "multi-dimensional programming combining quality video with quality print materials."

FedEx has one of the nation's most extensive satellite TV systems, which produces about 400 broadcasts annually—including a daily show for employees and managers—for more than 1,000 locations in the U.S., Canada, Great Britain and Europe. It also has an extensive publication system directed at all 85,000 employees—and at target audiences within that group. There are also special management publications.

Allstate Insurance Company also has a diversified internal communication system; its major emphasis is on the print media plus regular use of satellite videoconferencing for its management group.

It has a large stable of publications organized on a target-audience approach. Two corporate publications go to all employees at home. *Allstate Now* is a magazine published nine times a year. *Insight* is a quarterly newsletter which focuses on health and benefits issues.

The Bottom Line goes quarterly to 7,200 management people at work.

Also produced at the corporate level are publications for home office employees (a monthly); for agency personnel (a quarterly), for local communicators (a "how-to" advice quarterly), for retirees (a quarterly)—and there is a weekly news roundup transmitted elec-tronically to local offices.

Each of Allstate's three main business units—personal prop-erty and casualty, business, and life insurance—has its own employee publication. The forty local offices have newsletters, mostly bimonthly.

FACE-TO-FACE COMMUNICATION

In implementing an effective system of organizational communication, face-to-face discussions obviously should have top billing. This places heavy responsibility on every manager and supervisor to be as well informed as possible on company matters, and to be an on-going conduit for two-way sharing of information and ideas with employees. The success of supervisor-employee communication depends on the flow of quality information to managers from both corporate and local levels.

Face-to-Face in Smaller Organizations

In smaller organizations, face-to-face communication assumes even more importance when compared to other media. In many small operations, in fact, the personal approach by managers is best. Employees, both as individuals and in groups, can be handled almost exclusively—and very effectively—on a face-to-face basis.

Communication at All Levels

But the responsibility for face-to-face communication rests not only with supervisors who are working with their own employees, but with higher levels of managers, too. At each location, there should be a regular schedule of face-to-face meetings where employees have the opportunity to hear their top leaders discuss problems and goals, and to get answers concerning their questions and concerns. Some progressive managers hold meetings of this type every quarter, but twice a year is viewed as a more reasonable and practical target for most operations.

Each location also should encourage first-line supervisors to hold regular meetings with the people they supervise, ideally every quarter. Videotapes produced locally or at company headquarters can be extremely helpful in providing the foundation for discussions of priority subjects—quality, costs, competition, up-coming products, safety and environmental problems are obvious examples. Notes from staff meetings can also be valuable fodder for stimulating give-and-take discussions at these meetings.

Variety of Meeting Formats

Some corporate, group or divisional executives pride themselves on having what they call "diagonal-slice" or "general manager" meetings with employees whenever they visit outlying facilities. Others prefer to meet peer groups—hourly employees without managers, salaried employees without managers or supervisors with or without top-rung executives. A regular schedule of meetings between management and union leaders at various levels is also a desirable goal.

Properly conducted, regular face-to-face meetings of any variety between management and employees can provide a healthy exchange of complaints, concerns and ideas. They can be invigorating and educational, too, for both employees and management. Highlights of such meetings should be conveyed to the total employee group at these locations—the local employee publication is an ideal medium for doing this.

With higher-level executives—again if conducted properly in an open, informal, receptive and responsive manner—regular meetings with employees can help humanize the image of top executives. They can help convert the "fiery dragon" or "mysterious monarch" image of top executives to that of flesh-and blood "guys like us" who are working hard to make the company succeed.

EMPLOYEE SUGGESTION PLANS

Employee suggestion plans are viewed by some companies as an excellent medium for the upward communication of ideas for improving the business. Others believe that the existence of suggestion programs is an admission of weakness in the employee communication system and that the suggestion plan represents lip service to the cause of upward communication and legitimate employee participation.

Quite the contrary! In the first place, properly administered suggestion plans can represent substantial savings for a company. It is estimated, for example, that the General Motors program results in savings in excess of $700 million annually. In addition, advocates believe that suggestion plans represent an ideal way of inviting employees to contribute more to the organization's progress and to be recognized and rewarded for the effort.

Of course, the suggestion plan should only be view
part of a diversified employee communication plan. A
maintained as "just another ho-hum employee relations" bo   ⌐ ᴏ
not worth the time or effort expended. Obviously, the program
should be conducted efficiently with award decisions being made
promptly and on a basis which leans toward the employee in judging
value.

The Japanese are strong advocates of suggestion plans and
normally have participation of a large majority of their employees—
in the range of sixty to seventy percent. Their emphasis is on
securing a large number of small suggestions; in comparison, most
American plans spotlight the big money savers but usually achieve
a much smaller percentage of employee involvement.

If you could do all information-sharing on a face-to-face basis,
that would be ideal—immediate transmission, immediate feedback.
But obviously, other priorities don't permit that much personal time
for communicating. And frankly, a lot of managers still don't want
to spend the time on an activity that doesn't have potential for
immediate bottom-line results.

Also, even under the best conditions, the face-to-face network
occasionally breaks down or doesn't do the complete job. That's why
supplemental media must be organized to support and reinforce the
face-to-face information sharing that goes on every day—planned
and unplanned—in every organization.

So, let's examine the major formal media available for communicating with the total employee group.

PRINTED COMMUNICATION—THE OLD STANDBY

In the past, the employee communication programs, particularly
those involving publications, experienced serious difficulties because of their "house-organ" image—they were viewed as the obse-
quious panderer to management egos and whims.

Employee publications devoted much of their space to such
things as employee sports achievements, babies, service anniversa-
ries, retirements and classified ads. This is "unproductive garbage,"
informational trivia which makes little or no contribution to business goals or to priority employee information needs—unless the
organization is a social club.

In the past, too, many managers begrudgingly issued a newsletter once in a while and figured their communication responsibilities were all taken care of. In fact, that's still the case in many organizations—and as a result, the employee publication becomes a means of avoiding truly effective multimedia communication efforts. It's simply not a stand-alone method.

Significant Recent Gains in Publications

Employee publications, however, have come a long way in the last 10–20 years, assuming a much more important place in the management process of most business firms. There is a wide spectrum of formats—from simple newsletters to middle-of-the-road two-color tabloids, to luxurious full-color magazines that dazzle the eye and the imagination.

Much maligned and often the first targets for axing during difficult economic times, employee publications at many companies have undergone dramatic transformations which match the changing sophistication of the organizations they serve. As a result, the better publications concentrate on more serious business challenges, goals and plans—along with significant employee achievements at work or in the community.

But even employee stories should have strong orientation to the organization and its goals; they should not involve frivolous activities like summer canoeing trips down the Mississippi, campaign-button collections, or having babies. Quintuplets? Now, that's news anywhere.

While attractive graphics and layout designs add to the impact of employee publications, they cannot replace substance. Special care must be exercised in maintaining a sensible balance between the meat and the flavor of publication menus. Obviously, a luxurious, expensive-looking publication carrying stories about major cutbacks in personnel and budgets will probably draw a lot of criticism—and rightfully so.

Frequency—as with management publications—is critical for building a feeling of continuity, importance and credibility for employee publications. Ten to twelve issues a year is strongly recommended; anything less seriously detracts from the respect and confidence the publication will enjoy with employees.

Also, mailing the publication to employee homes is strongly preferred over work-place distribution. The employee has more time to read it at home, and surveys show that good publications also have significant family readership as well. In addition, home distribution adds a touch of dignity and respect to the publication and to employee families.

Strong Publication Support

The important role of publications has been emphasized repeatedly in results from employee communication surveys.

Studies by Towers, Perrin, Forster & Crosby at a variety of companies during the 1987–89 period showed that:

- Seventy percent of employees thoroughly read their publications,
- Ninety-five percent found company publications easy to read,
- Nearly ninety percent said they believed all or most of what they read, and
- On the negative side, only thirty-six percent consider their company publication as a primary source of information (down from forty-five percent in 1980), with a variety of face-to-face activities commanding greater respect from employees.

So, it's obvious that publications have a special place in the employee communication environment of the 1990s. But it is also clear that publications will have to work even harder to retain strong support among the employee public in a changing work environment.

Research shows an overlap of at least three-fourths in terms of what management wants employees to know about the business and what employees say they want to know. In similar fashion, employees zero in on the same areas of major challenges for the business as top-ranking executives—such as problems dealing with productivity, product quality, dealer service, manufacturing costs compared to principal competitors and the need of the company to make enough profits for investing adequately in the future.

This large area of common ground between management and employees simplifies one of the communicator's most critical jobs—that of selecting priority content. But this selection depends on solid reading of management thinking as well as on regular testing of employee opinions, all of it mixed in with a fair-sized serving of gut instinct.

Hewlett-Packard's Brad Whitworth makes a good point when he says that priorities also must take into account what is being said about the company and the industry in external media. Often, reporting in the external news channels is not balanced—particularly when there are negative aspects. As a result, the company's employee communication program must ensure that the company viewpoints get fair treatment—i.e., a more balanced report.

Editorial Policies

Establishing and updating editorial policies for publications is especially important, either at the company or group level, or as a joint agreement. Publications carry a major share of the total communication effort. Because they are covering a wide variety of subjects on a very frequent basis, they have the potential (and they run the risk) of making regular excursions into uncharted waters where company policy is nonexistent or under development.

Employee communicators have a moral obligation to speak for and protect employee interests.

In establishing editorial policies, the needs and desires of employees must be given top consideration, along with business priorities. Employee communicators have a moral obligation to speak for and protect employee interests, while also working hard to help achieve organizational goals. Honesty and clarity should be cardinal rules. The information-sharing process also should be regular and prompt in moving information, and it should consistently report both good news and bad.

Here's why:

- If publications don't have a solid share of editorial space devoted to news about the organization, don't expect management support when times are tough. Management will have no reasons to support the publication when dollars are in short supply.
- If breaking news of concern to employees isn't communicated promptly, management will be scooped by the grapevine or the news media—and maybe both.
- Reporting bad news is always difficult, but it is absolutely essential for credibility and should not be compromised.
- Strict adherence to schedules for certain types of written materials—such as newsletters, tabloids and electronic newslines—helps to establish reliability in the minds of employees.

Redundancies in Publication Networks

Efficiency experts continually raise questions about the number of employee publications. This is particularly true in larger organizations, where publications may be published at virtually every level of the organization. In some companies, for example, this means publications at corporate, group, divisional, plant and department levels—which may add up to several hundred publications. Obviously, there is a limit—from the standpoint of both information overload and cost—beyond which you have "rampant redundancy."

This is a very important question frequently raised in many companies, and it is one which deserves thoughtful consideration.

A corporate employee publication, for example, serves a unique and valuable purpose for both management and employees that cannot be satisfied from any other sources. There is also strong justification for publications and other communication media at every level of the organization.

This is true as long as the information has value to both management and/or employees and is, in its overall mass, directed to business goals, especially those of the local organization. Employee publications certainly can serve their own unique purposes by informing employees of the local unit's problems, plans and goals and by enhancing teamwork and esprit de corps. And, like advertising themes, there is proven merit to repetition of your messages when approached from different interest levels.

Allstate's Dick Madden is one who expresses concern about information overload:

> We get some strong reactions to volume. There are a lot of Allstate-generated information pieces which employees are expected to read and digest. When they go home at night, they are bombarded with radio and TV news; the coffee table is filled with magazines and newspapers. If we're giving them six or so additional things on top of all the rest, they just aren't going to read it. We've lost them.

Certainly, information overload is a potentially serious problem for many organizations. But the concern should be more about quality than quantity. Of major importance are the substance and relativity of the information to employees and the quality of the writing—with conciseness and clarity being prime requirements.

In the final analysis, is the publication network cost-effective? Are the publications getting the company's messages across and, through localization, making them more meaningful to employees, wherever they are in the organization?

Getting Best Value Is Goal. Integration of corporate and local publications represents one possible solution. An outside or inside four-page spread from corporate level could provide priority corporate information for a company's local publications structured on a common format—such as an eight-page format—but also allow for strong local input in the rest of the publication. Such systems present serious problems in terms of matching quality of content and writing, and also logistical nightmares in timing, production and distribution. But it can be done.

Local editorial freedom is, of course, a highly desirable goal. But with the tough economics of most organizations nowadays, better integration or coordination of total print communications should be a way of life in seeking maximum value for investments in employee publication networks.

In summary, employee publications in multi-location organizations represent a high-potential communication network which reaches into the very heart of organizations. Even in decentralized operations, there is a need for overall direction, coordination and professional assistance from the corporate level, assistance which ensures the maximum effectiveness of efforts toward both local and corporate business goals.

Is There a Future for Joint Publications?

The subject of joint employee publications—the sharing of editorial responsibilities between management and unions—can stimulate strong feelings on both sides. And even within company ranks, there are also strong disagreements about whether joint publications can provide more two-sided, honest communication for employees.

GM's Allan Csiky believes that many of his company's employee publications have regressed in trying to practice jointness in the past.

> The problem isn't the concept of "jointness" as a partnership; a true partnership is powerful. Too often, however, the execution doesn't match the ideal.
>
> Any story gets muddier and weaker when you negotiate how to say it. Often, unions still don't trust management, and vice versa. It can be slower and harder to be honest and candid because the unions have their sacred cows, too. My chief criticism of joint publications is that there is a tendency to focus on form (how many column inches each side gets) and too little concern for honest content. The "victims" are the same—the employees who can quickly spot "pap" whether in management, union or joint forms.

In some cases, the joint publication concept has worked well and the final result is a strong, meaty publication that softens the propaganda aspects of both management and unions and projects objective, credible information for employees. But by their very nature, joint publications are tied into the political process between management and unions, and as such they are subject to rough seas and even elimination if that's the way the political winds blow.

Politics Scrap GM's Joint Publications. "There is always a risk in the joint relationship," Csiky points out.

> What if one partner has a change of heart...or has a change of leadership? That's what happened at GM when Steve Yokich replaced Don Ephlin as UAW vice president in charge of the GM department. Yokich apparently doesn't share Ephlin's enthusiasm for joint publications and they quickly disappeared in General Motors—at least at the higher levels. The whole episode didn't demonstrate a very strong commitment on anybody's part to communicate with employees, although plants that had constructive and major joint communication efforts continued them.

GM's first major employee publication to go joint was *Working,* a monthly tabloid publication of the Buick-Oldsmobile-Cadillac (B-O-C) Group which was launched in close cooperation with the GM department of the United Auto Workers Union in 1986. Over a 3-year period, this 110,000-circulation publication built a solid reputation among employees for presenting both sides of major business happenings.

Working was so successful that by early 1989, with encouragement from both union and management brass, GM's other major operations were in the process of converting group employee publications to joint efforts.

However, these plans changed abruptly when Steve Yokich took over as vice president in charge of the UAW's GM department in the spring of 1989. Yokich made it clear that joint publications (and other joint management-union strategies) were not on his agenda, which called for a tougher, more confrontational relationship with GM.

B-O-C executives say *Working* will continue to be a true employee publication as far as they can go, even without the union as a partner. Editor Karen Healy says the task will be more difficult in some respects.

> The UAW brought a different perspective to *Working.* Looking at a particular subject through two sets of eyes helped make our stories more balanced, more complete, perhaps more honest in the eyes of our readers. We learned a lot from our joint relationship and expect to use this experience to continue *Working* as a top-notch employee publication.

Joint publications have to walk a razor-thin line: In presenting both sides of issues, they must be careful not to anger either side with unreasonable criticism. On the other hand, if they present only issues on which management and unions agree, they lose their value as a forum for explaining major disagreements to employees. But few managements will pay the bill for publications that are destructively critical of their top executives.

Only time will tell if this new type of "editorial alliance" will gain broader acceptance as a means of representing the key interests of both management and unions. Or will it become another example of the phenomenon that almost never the twain will meet in union-management relations?

Special Publications

In recent years, two new types of publications have evoked increased attention and discussion in the corporate world—the retiree publication and the employee annual report.

Retiree Publications. In the past, most people who had served companies in long and distinguished careers were honored with farewell parties, given a service watch, told what their pension and benefits were, and promptly forgotten. With increasing national longevity, however, the country's retiree group represents a source of both political clout and potential support for American institutions. In some established businesses, in fact, the number of retirees is expected to surpass the number of active employees by the mid—1990s.

This has resulted in new activities by most organizations aimed at keeping retirees up-to-date on company developments, problems and plans. These activities also seek to solicit their support in such areas as stock ownership and product purchases and proposed government regulations at both the national and local levels.

The typical retiree publication—quarterly or bimonthly in most cases—has already become a fundamental channel for communicating with retirees. In many companies, the typical retiree publication is similar to the organization's corporate employee publication because it uses some common editorial materials and is done by the employee communication staff.

Employee Annual Reports. Employee annual reports almost beg an answer to the question: "Why?" But they have sprung up like mushrooms in recent years to fill a recognition vacuum in employee-management relations.

Most employees, in major companies at least, are also stockholders, either through stock-purchase saving plans or personal purchases of stock. So, if they already get the organization's annual report, why do they need another one?

Advocates of the employee annual report say that most companies don't really give enough credit to employee achievements in the official annual report. While that's a corporate shame, it's probably true that most annual reports patronize and stroke employees at best—and ignore them, except in statistics, at worst.

Certainly many company annual reports are highly technical and difficult to read, obviously written with no real regard for typical employees. The prime audiences clearly are stockholders and financial analysts, not employees.

So again the question is asked: "Why?"

Lawrence Ragan examined the pros and cons of employee annual reports in a 1989 series of articles in his weekly newsletter for communicators, *The Ragan Report,* a series which generated a lot of reader comments.[1]

Ragan says that most people appear to support some kind of simplified annual report, one which is written for employees in a language they can understand and which stresses the things that are most important to them as employees.

One of the weaknesses in many current reports, Ragan says, is that they don't have a proper balance of company and employee achievements. "Without a frank recognition of current business problems, employee achievements stand in a vacuum," he points out.

He suggests that making them a part of—or a special insert in—the regular employee publication might be a solution which satisfies the most reasons for doing an employee publication.

Ragan says that another solution being considered by a growing number of corporations, is to make annual report time an occasion for doing a more complete communication package. This might include the use of several media, such as a special publication aimed at employees, videotaped highlights for use by supervisors in discussions with employees and visual summaries of the annual meeting.

Whatever the arguments against employee annual reports, they have already become part of the corporate communication culture, and each year brings more advances in their special state-of-the-art contribution. As the American work place becomes more participative, employee annual reports will require increasing attention from communication managers.

FILMS AND VIDEOTAPES

Many companies make good use of film and videotapes in communication activities for all employees. But their greatest potential

[1] *Ragan Reports* (Chicago), issues of June 5 and July 17, 24 and 31, 1989.

appears to be as vehicles for supervisors to use in regular meetings with the people they supervise.

IBM produces about fifty videotapes a year which are designed for both management and employee viewing and which feature company news, executive interviews and personnel-type subjects. Highlights of management conferences are produced for showing to all employees, and a package of supplementary teacher's-guide materials are provided to assist managers.

IBM also has a sizable library of videotapes available for employee use—at work or to take home for viewing—which focus special attention on both personnel topics and an assortment of health subjects such as smoking, drug abuse and exercise. Some of them are produced by IBM, but most are purchased from outside sources.

Problems with Videotapes, Films

The use of films and videotapes for communicating with all employees involves some serious problems: Lost production time is a major concern. Taking employees off the job for an hour once or twice a year represents a substantial expenditure of money—even for those who consider good communication a solid investment.

On the positive side, there are many managers who maintain that they get back every hour devoted to solid video communication in increased productivity and employee understanding. The substance and quality of the video/film productions make a big difference.

Johnson & Johnson produces about sixty videotapes a year—primarily for management—but most can be shown to all employees if local management desires. But J&J's Larry Foster has some reservations about the use of video, particularly for communicating with all employees.

> Compared with print, video is by far the more difficult medium to evaluate. It is more expensive to produce, requires more staff time and resources, and is hard to assess with regard to cost versus benefits. One of the problems is finding time in the work day for employees to watch video programs. Managers are understandably reluctant to halt production lines and interrupt office work to watch video programs unless they are part of a training project. Therefore, we must be very selective in programs we ask managers to show to all employees.

If films or videotapes contain hard-hitting facts of the business—if they discuss things like high labor costs or the need for reduced expenses in labor or benefit costs—they can create problems with the unions. They could even evoke threats of boycott or work stoppages.

Political Power Censorship. This happened to General Motors in 1982, when union pressure resulted in the cancellation of a 20-minute film entitled "Road to Survival." Among other things, the film featured a comparison of labor costs for GM and the Japanese auto industry. Although prior to that time, annual state-of-the-business films had gained wide acceptance among management and employees alike, the 1982 union threats essentially eliminated the use of films for showing to all employees in GM.

It was a classic example of political power censorship. In later years, even the mention of the possibility of a new film for all employees sent trembles through labor-relations ranks.

The ideal solution to problems with the unions would involve two actions by employee communicators. First, make sure that presentation of sensitive or controversial information is done as objectively as possible. And second, try to secure the cooperation of union officials in putting the materials together, inviting them to appear in the productions and to participate in discussion periods following video/film presentations.

Some local managers object to pressures for use of corporate films or videotapes which don't contain a great deal of substance relating directly to local operations. Local managers rightly feel that the real focus should be on local problems and goals. They also point out with emphasis that "our employees can't ask questions of a videotape. Supply us with the important corporate information and we'll include it in our own presentations."

CLOSED-CIRCUIT TELEVISION

About ten years ago, I participated in a Public Relations Society of America seminar in Chicago where the speaker preceding me said that videoconferencing and closed-circuit television (CCTV) were going to make print media as useless as six-foot centers in the National Basketball Association.

My strong objections probably made me sound very old-fashioned, but I predicted that during the rest of my own career, print media would remain the old standby.

If I only had been as prophetic about the stock market!

Closed-circuit TV has been around for quite a while—and it was highly over-glamorized in its early years. CCTV connects a number of locations in the same geographic area by cable and can distribute video programs to multiple TV monitors simultaneously. It allows for live studio presentations as well as use of videotapes or films. It sounds great thus far.

However, in most places where I have seen CCTV put into use, not enough thought was given to the tremendous sophistication required to produce network-quality productions—and anything less loses audiences, even among managers. Employees are seasoned viewers of top-quality TV, and anything significantly less than that is simply not acceptable.

Too often when CCTV systems are established, not enough attention is given to the quality or quantity of personnel requirements or to the insatiable appetite of TV systems. CCTV systems are often installed by plant engineers without counsel from employee communication experts, and they are thrust into the plants as colorful, exotic entities rather than as one part of a multi-faceted communication program.

Technology alone can't solve any communication problem.

For anyone considering CCTV as a main channel for employee communication, it is critical that the financial, personnel and equipment requirements be evaluated thoroughly—also factor in the availability of up-to-date videotape materials from within the organization and outside. And remember that if you decide to take employees off their jobs to watch CCTV shows, that's lost production and therefore expensive. So the programs have to be substantive to be worth the cost—not just a case of amateur TV producers having fun.

Also, TV monitors placed in break areas or cafeterias, in my opinion, are more show pieces than effective channels of communication. They're limited by what they can effectively communicate (difficulty in hearing is a big handicap), and they are an infringement on the relaxation time of employees.

So, if you're thinking about CCTV, make sure you have a thorough evaluation of all the human and equipment requirements and visit some organizations that have tried closed-circuit TV successfully or have failed.

SATELLITE TELEVISION

Earlier, we discussed the outstanding potential for using satellite television for communicating with the management group, particularly in organizations with broad geographic dispersion of operations. I do not have the same enthusiasm about its use for communicating corporate information to *all* employees.

The reasons for my reservations are generally the same as with film and videotape, particularly if the informational materials involve hard-hitting, honest, high-quality productions. These obstacles are union objections, cost of taking employees off the job and the reluctance of local managers to use corporate videos in place of their own localized presentations.

Advocates of private television cite rapid advances in technology; lower costs for equipment, production and distribution; and the globalization of many organizations. But it is not the cost of internal TV which is the big obstacle; it is the expense of taking employees off their jobs for sit-down showings.

From a competitive standpoint, television offers the potential of bringing top company executives face-to-face with employees on a more personal, candid, simultaneous basis in plants, offices and warehouses all over the world. It has the potential of focusing a person's attention on the message it is delivering as no other medium can.

There are some significant potential advances in technology now being explored which feature multiple meetings of small groups of people at considerably less cost than satellite transmission. Some companies are experimenting with set-up rooms capable of two-way audio and two-way video using telephone lines for transmission; in such rooms full-motion video is now possible. And public rooms are available worldwide through commercial service companies.

These systems allow for meetings involving multiple locations (as many as twenty-five)—with as many as twelve people at each location. They are ideal for small group problem solving and the cost savings over satellite transmissions are significant. This opens up new opportunities, not to replace videoconferencing for large group transmissions, but to supplement it for more specialized purposes.

As in many aspects of mass communication, there are differing opinions about the value of specific media. The use of TV for communicating with all employees is one of those areas.

Major Corporations Big on TV

Ford Motor Company is a strong believer in the television medium and has invested heavily in equipment and resources to give it a top-notch capability in this field. Ford plans to use satellite TV for a variety of informational programs for all employees. But significant emphasis will be on special communication packages for management groups—on a variety of subjects and at every level, including important first-level supervisors. (See Case Example 9 on Ford's TV system at the end of this chapter on pages 154-57.)

Federal Express also has a very extensive satellite television system for employee communication, a system with more than 1,000 downlinks in the U.S., Canada, Great Britain & Europe and 400-plus broadcasts a year. Its program places heavy emphasis on job-related information, including daily business updates, discussion of recurring-problem areas and ideas for improving performance at all levels.

A Week in TV at AT&T

AT&T's Ray O'Connell used a week in October 1989 to demonstrate the value and diversity of satellite TV in communicating with both managers and employees:

- *October 16.* Jim Florio, successful Democratic candidate for governor of New Jersey, was featured in a Q&A session for a large employee audience at the Basking Ridge headquarters, a program broadcast live to twenty-three AT&T locations in the state. (Republican candidate Jim Courter got the honors the following week.)
- *October 18.* A nationwide press conference on the actions taken to maintain the AT&T network in the aftermath of the San Francisco earthquake was broadcast to news reporters assembled in company facilities and also to network management and thousands of AT&T employees

engaged in disaster recovery operations. Footage from the telecast was also picked up by many commercial TV stations.

- *October 19.* AT&T Chairman Bob Allen participated in a telecast discussion of a special early retirement program for viewing by 100,000 managers at some 250 U.S. locations.

AT&T produces about fifty live broadcasts per year for employees, involving mainly productions for major business units. Most deal with personnel issues and involve telephone call-in questions which are answered during the telecasts.

AT&T has about 300 permanent downlinks in North American locations—and this number continues to grow. For occasional overseas needs, equipment is rented.

In targeting audiences for AT&T TV programs, the rifle is replacing the shotgun. The trend is toward what O'Connell calls "narrowcasting"—aiming programs at specific groups of employees with some common interest. It may be geographical (the public affairs programs for New Jersey employees) or organizational (the head of a business unit or division reporting to nationally-deployed people in that unit).

Trend to More Operational Telecasts

AT&T also now broadcasts live press conferences announcing new products especially for employees who have the responsibility for selling, installing or maintaining those products.

O'Connell says:

AT&T's TV menu in the past year or so has become more operational than informational. The information we provide helps employees do their jobs better rather than being of broad, general interest. It's bottom-line oriented.

TV is a high-impact medium which needs to be used sparingly. When people are asked to view a broadcast, they need to know that the subject is important to them personally or will improve their job performance—a time-enhancer, not a time-waster. Getting this kind of information must not be perceived as an add-on frill, but as a basic part of their jobs. To maintain that level of integrity, you need to be rigorously selective about the subjects you choose for live TV treatment.

IBM is also moving aggressively into broadcast television, with plans for a network of up to 800 U.S. downlinks—with two-way audio at some key locations. Monitors will be located in public areas and conference facilities will be at all locations.

Les Simon, IBM's U.S. communications vice president, says plans call for a daily morning TV show (about 5 minutes in length) and special features (15–20 minutes) as regular programming for the network. Live coverage of major events such as news conferences, new product introductions and executive-interview shows will add substance and credibility to the process. It is also expected that IBM's major business units will make regular use of this resource in communicating with their employees, management and customers.

Allstate's Dick Madden, who directs an extensive print network along with quarterly management videoconferences, believes his company will expand the use of TV for communicating with all employees on some issues in the future.

> The 1990s will see increasing awareness among professionals to gear up communication activities to match the format and quality of what employees can get in their homes—toward more emphasis on the passive media, radio and TV. With our younger employees particularly, who grew up with TV, it's the medium they're most comfortable with and are inclined to pay attention to. More and more, that's our competition in communicating effectively with employees.

EXECUTIVE VISITS TO FIELD OPERATIONS

Now, let's look at a high-potential communication medium, but one that's largely ignored by many organizations. That's personal visits by top corporate executives to local operations, and the scheduling of informal talks with employees and/or managers while on location.

It goes almost without saying that employees expect their own top managers to circulate through local operations on a regular basis—chatting with employees, listening to problems or concerns. It's not necessary to solve major problems in such wandering-around. But most experts believe that amiable, friendly contact with employees on a regular basis can do much to dispel the negative impressions created by a management invisible in its own work places.

Employees Want to Hear It from Top Executives

If you have any doubts about the high value which employees place on communication from top company executives, multi-company TPF&C surveys in the 1987–89 period should allay your concerns.

When asked to specify current sources for company information, only fifteen percent of employees list their company's top executives as a primary source. However, sixty-two percent of the employees preferred the organization's top executives as a primary source—an expectation or disappointment gap of forty-seven percent. In the same studies, fifty-nine percent said their immediate supervisors were a primary source and a preferred source of ninety percent—a disappointment gap of thirty-one percent.

So, while the immediate supervisor still rates number one as the actual and preferred source of information, look at the tremendous potential revealed when nearly two-thirds of the employees said they preferred top management, but most of them had to go elsewhere to get their information about the company.

Few Companies Send Many Officers Out

As far as executive visits to outlying facilities are concerned, the top two or three executives in many companies do make serious efforts to visit a number of plants or offices each year. And certainly these top executives can't take on unlimited schedules of facility visits and still carry out their full-time responsibilities at home.

In some companies, executives of groups and divisions visit their own operations regularly. The most effective format would include talks to at least a representative group of supervisors and/or employees—and a lot of wandering around to talk personally with employees and union officials.

But from my observations and experience, there are not nearly enough companies which capitalize on this potential—and this is particularly true of corporate officers other than the chief executive and president. As a result, top corporate leadership remains aloof and almost invisible to employees in many companies. And the bigger the company, the bigger the problem.

Visits Should Be Done Well, Honestly

It is critical, however, that visits be done well, and honestly. They can't be quick fly-throughs, with motorized carts whisking "the brass" around like royalty. And if the top people don't visit company facilities on some kind of regular basis, it's a mistake to rush them around to a few key plants on the eve of labor negotiations. Employees see this for what it is, and the value of the face-to-face interaction with employees is greatly reduced.

The least believable scenario has the CEO making a half-dozen whistle stops (once every three years) at plants critical to new contract labor negotiations—accompanied by an entourage which includes the company's labor relations vice president, the plant manager and the chairman of the union shop committee.

Care also should be taken not to intimidate employees; informality and personal warmth are important. But perhaps most of all, visiting dignitaries should be serious about listening to employee concerns, engaging in personal discussions as much as possible, and getting back to employees with answers not delivered on the spot.

A regular agenda of facility visits can pump a lot of personal warmth and confidence into the traditional cold-blooded image which many employees have of corporate executives. It also gives central office executives an opportunity to update themselves with exposure to the first-hand, up-to-date feelings of the company at the ground level.

When company executives visit outlying offices and plants and talk to employees and supervisors individually and in groups, they are demonstrating good communication by example. And their actions say to associates and subordinates: "If this is important enough for me to take the time to communicate on a face-to-face basis, you should too."

Publicizing Visits and Discussions

Reporting the highlights of such visits and discussions in local and corporate media will serve to broaden substantially the impact of such face-to-face communication throughout the total organization.

Chevron Corporation takes advantage of visits by its top executives to cities where the company has sizable installations by adding discussion sessions with employees. These sessions, which are called "Town Hall" meetings, are very informal in format. The chairman or president speaks from notes for 10–15 minutes and then answers questions from employees for up to an hour, during which time anything goes. Following stockholder meetings, Chevron also has produced videotaped highlights from "Town Hall" sessions for distribution to all Chevron locations.

It should be a primary responsibility of the employee communication manager to recommend a reasonable schedule of visits to field locations by top company executives, and to secure special training and speech materials for such activities. It is also important to brief the top executives on local issues; it indicates understanding and empathy for problems and concerns of local management and employees.

BEATING THE GRAPEVINE AND EXTERNAL NEWS MEDIA

How about the grapevine and the external news media?

Research consistently shows that only a small percentage of employees prefer getting their information from these two sources. They also rate them much lower in believability, particularly the grapevine, when compared to management sources. But about two-thirds of the employees also say they get their information through these two sources before they get it through official channels.

The challenge to communicators is clear: Organize a communication system that moves with speed, accuracy and completeness and which reaches employees first—at least most of the time.

The grapevine is almost impossible to beat. There's too many people handling information involved in the decision-making process, including its administrative aspects. But once the decision is made, speed in moving the news through official channels is paramount if the grapevine is to be silenced before it runs amuck with snowballing rumors. But not all grapevine information is wrong or distorted; it can also confirm the truth.

Regardless of how the grapevine is viewed as a medium for communicating information, its value as a feedback source should not be overlooked. It can give almost immediate feedback on management actions and serve as an early warning predictor of reactions to upcoming actions.

If the news is of primary interest to employees (such as layoffs; office, lab or plant closings; or a new top executive), adequate time should be allowed for managers to speak personally with their people. And they should be able to do so prior to the time the announcements are made through internal communication channels and outside news media. If an electronic newsline is available, the news should be dispatched to internal sites before it is given to newspapers, radio and TV—or at least at the same time.

In short, an effective employee communication system should be able to beat the grapevine some of the time and the news media almost all of the time. Employees will applaud efforts to achieve these goals.

SUMMARY

Face-to-face meetings and publications are the most effective media for sharing corporate materials with all employees. Publications, videotapes and satellite TV are the media of greatest potential for sharing information with management. Most management publications and videotapes should be shared by supervisors with their employees—even the most confidential ones, at local management discretion.

It is also strongly recommended that local operations produce their own publications, videotapes, films or letters—and that they make use of bulletin boards or other local outlets. Some locations, which have the equipment and technical expertise, may find closed-circuit TV an effective medium. But careful evaluation is recommended before investing heavily in this medium.

The important point is that each organization or location should decide, after thorough analysis, which mix of media serves its own communication needs most effectively. The proof is in the pudding; results will tell you when you have the right combination.

CASE 9

At Ford Motor Company

TELEVISION
IS A BIG-TIME
COMMUNICATOR

Television is being developed as a major tool for communicating with employees at the Ford Motor Company, both in North American and off-shore operations. And the company has made a substantial investment in equipment (industry estimates say well over $10 million) and in top TV professionals to capitalize on the full potential of this medium.

Jack Caldwell, director of internal communications on the Ford public affairs staff, had 30 years of broadcast experience before going to Ford; in his last job he was president and general manager of Detroit's Public Broadcasting Service station.

COMMUNICATION IS COMPETITIVE ASSET

Top Ford executives believe that good employee communication—including a strong core of TV—represents a definite competitive asset. They guard some aspects of their internal communication strategy as jealously as they do future car designs.

Since going to Ford in 1983, Caldwell has been responsible for organizing various company video resources and for modernizing production and editing facilities for use in both internal and external communication activities. The TV system, along with internal print materials, is included in the Ford Communication Network (FCN). A monthly tabloid newspaper—*Ford World*—is mailed to employee homes and is the company's major print communication vehicle.

Ford has full- or part-time communicators at each of more than 200 North American locations, and they are responsible for both TV and print communication activities. Conferences for this group are held every 2 years in Dearborn for training and exchange of information. Plans are to hold several additional conferences each year—via interactive television.

The headquarters FCN staff is available to assist divisional, plant and staff units with video productions. FCN is aggressively encouraging greater use of "custom-designed video information packages" for employees and for all groups or levels of management people.

While Ford says the current level of such productions involving FCN is proprietary information, industry sources say it is significant. Reports that the company has contacts with about l00 individual freelance video professionals during a year's production cycle attests to a sizable production schedule. And annual increases of at least ten percent in production output are expected over the next few years.

Essentially all of Ford's North American manufacturing facilities and zone-sales offices—more than 280—are equipped to receive one-way video signals from the Dearborn world headquarters. More than sixty of these sites, based in Dearborn, are reached via commercial cable, and the rest via satellite. All Dearborn locations have origination capabilities to connect with domestic and international satellites.

More than twenty-five locations in North America have two-way compressed video transmission capabilities. Major plant locations also are equipped with closed-circuit TV.

THREE REGULAR PROGRAMS ON SATELLITE TV

At the company level, FCN has regularly scheduled TV programs delivered via satellite and cable TV:

- An around-the-clock text news service that takes about 5 minutes to read; updated regularly, throughout the day.

- A 5-minute newscast 5 days a week designed for rebroadcast in plant and zone locations every hour.

- A monthly 15-minute TV magazine primarily designed for taping and later use for a variety of activities, including management viewing, supervisory use with employees or in training sessions.

Subjects for the daily newscasts include auto shows, sales and profit reports, company developments around the world, employee achievements and excerpts from major executive speeches. Caldwell says:

Our telecasts have to compete with commercial TV news programs in terms of quality and credibility. If we are too self-serving in content; if we don't cover both good and bad news, or if we feature top Ford executives too much, employees will turn us off—or worse yet, they won't believe us. We try to be as open, as candid and as professional as possible; it's the only way.

The monthly 15-minute TV programs probe deeper into major issues facing Ford. Typical subjects have included:

- Japanese plants in the U.S.
- The U.S. economy, its impact on Ford and vice versa.
- Outsourcing—i.e., why Ford must do some buying of products and components overseas to remain competitive.
- The need for profitability.
- Building a major plant in Hermosillo, Mexico.

EARLY CONCERNS ALL BUT DISAPPEARED

Caldwell says discussing stories like these—particularly subjects like the Hermosillo plant and outsourcing—initially created serious concerns within the company. "But things are much better now," he says.

We have an enlightened management which agrees with the need to communicate on an honest, timely basis with employees even on the so-called sensitive subjects. It was a culture change we had to go through; but we're well along that road now and the concerns of middle managers have all but disappeared.

FCN also broadcasts a number of special events each year—such as the annual stockholders meeting, which is covered from gavel to gavel. Important press conferences also are carried live on satellite TV—about six to seven per year. Examples of broadcast events are quarterly earnings reports, new product offerings and special product-award ceremonies. Highlights of other press conferences are included in the daily TV newscasts.

Caldwell says that TV viewing, "even in small bites over time, can create a healthy perspective for employees—a broad understanding of what the company is, what we do, our economics, our products, our culture, our attitude and our determination to win—these things will come through."

QUALITY AND EFFICIENCY ARE KEY GOALS

Efficiency is a prime goal at FCN, along with quality of productions. Ford makes heavy use of freelancers in producing its videos. Caldwell says his total production costs must match those of the highly competitive video business in Detroit.

> As we originally mapped plans for broader information sharing with employees, it was obvious that Ford's senior management recognized the value of an informed work force and also the need for an efficient news-gathering and distribution system. With that type of support, FCN was able to move aggressively in making itself a recognized part of the core management circle.
>
> As a result, the task of informing employees about the company, its products and customers, competition and the competitive environment is now a process that is everybody's job at Ford. When you know how you stand against the competition, you know what you must do to win.

Caldwell expects increasing use of TV not only at corporate headquarters, but also by corporate staffs, operating divisions and plant locations.

> Employees want much more than company information; they also want to know how their own staff or plant is doing. They want to know how local problems and goals translate into increased responsibilities, opportunities and security for them.
>
> We want to become the best company in the world, however you want to measure it. We are committed to the belief that our success in part hinges on how well we communicate among ourselves. And we have the trust, confidence and support of the very top people in this company to carry out that mandate.

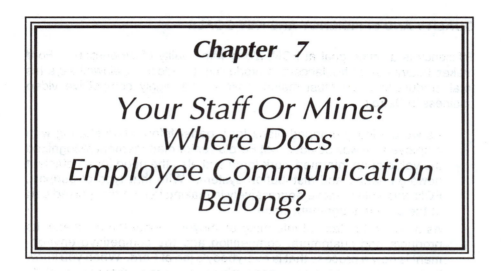

Chapter 7

Your Staff Or Mine? Where Does Employee Communication Belong?

One of the most frequent questions from professionals is whether employee communication functions better as a part of the public relations (corporate communication or public affairs) or personnel (human resources) staffs.

It seems as though everybody believes in communicating. Certainly, there are an unbelievable number of "experts" in our companies who want to tell communicators how to do their jobs. But the question is which staff is better qualified, has better resources and has the stronger fundamental motivation to do an honest job of communicating with employees.

On the surface at least, the answer is neither—and both.

In companies with traditional organizational structures and philosophy, neither the public relations staff nor the personnel staff is ideally suited to do the job in a way which serves the best interests of both employees and management.

TRENDS IN OWNERSHIP

Of the seventeen companies who contributed information for this part of the book, the employee communication function is on the public relations, public affairs or corporate communication staffs of sixteen companies and on the personnel staff of only one company.

A 1989 employee communication study by the Wyatt Company indicated that the trend is to place this responsibility in the human resources area. Personnel involvement increased from forty-six to fifty-three percent since 1986, while public relations' responsibility dropped from thirty-eight to thirty percent. In companies with 10,000 or more employees, the ratio favors public relations over personnel by fifty-three to thirty-four percent, relatively unchanged since 1986.

The Wyatt study was heavily oriented toward smaller companies and to the human resources area. Fifty-six percent of participating companies had 1,000 employees or fewer and more than half of the respondents were in the personnel/compensation/benefits areas compared to fifteen percent in the communication field. [1]

Bob Ellis, senior communication consultant for the Wyatt Company, says his firm's report indicates an obvious trend toward placing this function into the human resources area, regardless of company size. But, he adds, "the bigger the company, the more likely it is that the employee communication function will be housed outside of the human resources area."

A somewhat different conclusion was reached in a 1989 survey by the *PR Reporter* which showed public relations responsibility for employee communication at 70 percent compared to 22 percent for human resources. In contrast to the Wyatt emphasis on personnel, this study was oriented toward PR professionals in 841 participating companies which represented a wide range of sizes. [2]

It appears obvious that in the larger companies, the trend is to retain employee communication as a part of corporate communications. Many smaller companies are paying more attention to employee communication. But—and this is true in plant locations of large corporations, too—the function is being handled by a personnel professional, often as a lower-level priority on a part-time basis.

PERSONNEL STAFFS NEED GOOD COMMUNICATION

Personnel or human resources staffs have a great need for good employee communication in convincing employees of the high level of compensation and benefits they enjoy, in explaining personnel

---

[1] "Results of 1989 Wyatt Communication Survey," in *THE WYATT COMMU-NICATOR*, published by the Wyatt Company, June 1989, pp. 4–6.

[2] *PR Reporter*, weekly newsletter published by the PR Publishing Company, Exeter, N.H., January 22, 1990, p. 1.

policies and procedures, and in interpreting company actions in terms of their impact on employees.

Much of the personnel-type communication at most companies is handled through the organizational structure, largely by management and personnel directors at each staff, plant and office location, and much of it face-to-face. But established employee communication channels—such as publications, films and TV activities—are used to supplement face-to-face communication and further enhance employee understanding, loyalty and morale.

But there is an even more compelling demand for today's human resources executive to go beyond personnel policies, development and benefits in helping the manager achieve greater success in forging an understanding, cooperative, productive employee team. Effective communication between managers and employees is essential to this goal, of making free and honest sharing of information with employees a part of the basic fabric of management-employee relations. (GM's joint venture with Toyota to produce passenger cars at Fremont, California is based on this principle and has recorded outstanding success, as discussed in Case Example 10 at the end of this chapter on pages 171-75.)

To an increasing degree, personnel executives recognize the value of good communication and want the function to be carried out in a highly professional manner. And they are aggressive in making sure that priority personnel information ranks high on the communication agenda—wherever the function is located.

PROBLEMS WITH BOTH PERSONNEL AND PUBLIC RELATIONS

Some personnel people, however, have real problems in dealing with the practice of full disclosure, two-way communication with all employees using a mass-media approach. Those with long careers under autocratic management systems and restrictive information policies find it difficult to convert to an open-communication style.

They can stay in their comfort zone by saying, "Tell employees as little as you have to. 'Need to know' is the best rule." They have special difficulties dispensing negative news. Modifications in benefit plans, for example, are often couched in cumbersome, evasive technical language and with great flourish in a Barnum & Bailey style which says, "You never had it so good."

Some public relations people *also* have problems in giving internal communication a proper place in their priorities.

PR and corporate communication staffs generally are driven by the media relations function—which is directed to powerful external audiences. Because of their strong role in interpreting management actions and policies for the public media, news relations people are often viewed as acting out of the CEO's office. Other top executives, especially those who are regular spokespersons for the company, also recognize the importance of maintaining good relations with external news media.

As a result, PR staffs generally are inclined to rank a company's internal public at a lower priority—usually below the news media, stockholders and financial analysts.

GM Tried It Both Ways

General Motors is ideally suited to answering the question of whether employee communication belongs on the personnel or public relations staffs. It's tried it both ways, and its experience may provide some insight for other companies faced with the same dilemma.

For General Motors, it all started in late 1971 when the seeds for a modern employee communication system were planted. This system was to play a key part in a revolutionary concept of organization development, one launched with a long-term goal of bringing management, employees and unions together into a more enlightened, cooperative working relationship. Its objectives were improved teamwork, production and product quality, along with a more participative, satisfying work environment for all employees.

This was a dream of mammoth proportions, in which communication was to play a critical role. Key supporters of the new "human-resources" philosophy believed it could be successfully integrated into the company's worldwide organizational structure only if all employees had a solid understanding of this new philosophy, including its goals and the range of techniques available for achieving these goals. Equally important was the need to equip employees with a better understanding of the business itself—its problems, challenges and opportunities—as well as of their own roles in achieving local and corporate objectives.

This was the genesis of a modern employee communication system for General Motors, one with obvious potential for a corporation seeking major improvements in its management style. GM's employee communication efforts at that time were meager and amateurish; now there was a chance to begin with a clean sheet of paper. But the new system's tenure within the personnel structure was a disaster.

Personnel Executives Didn't Understand Communication. Top personnel executives simply did not recognize the importance of the new communication activity and of how it could contribute to the success of their mission. They were afraid to tell employees the whole truth. A "need-to-know" philosophy prevailed. They wanted to control information content, they wanted to talk only about the good side of the news and they wanted to restrict distribution of sensitive information to a few thousand executives. Their formula: skinny menus and only bland, sweet morsels, please.

Public relations executives also bristled over the creation of a second communication function within the corporation—and on another staff at that.

During a period of economic downturn in 1974–75, manpower for the fledgling department was cut in half and expenses were virtually brought to a complete halt. Three years of solid research had provided the basis for a comprehensive long-range strategic plan for a corporate-wide employee communication system. Unfortunately, it had been bottled up in the personnel administration and development staff.

PR Staff Moved Aggressively. However, the critical need persisted.

As a result, the responsibility for employee communication—along with its key professionals—was transferred to the public relations staff in 1975. Sixteen days later, the strategic plan which had collected cobwebs in the personnel administration and development staff for more than a year was approved by the executive vice president for finance and public affairs, Roger Smith, who was destined to be the next chairman of GM.

Once the responsibility was shifted, the public relations staff took strong action, which included:

- Organizing a series of thirty-three presentations on the new plan to more than 500 executives across the nation,

- Approving corporate policy and guidelines for management,
- Establishing basic communication channels such as a daily electronic newsline, a monthly tabloid publication, annual state-of-the-business films, and later, a whole series of special management communication activities.

In addition, the staff received a mandate from top corporate and public relations management to sell the program aggressively. But most important, it encountered a receptive management attitude on future improvements—and it was granted the budget and personnel needed to handle these improvements, on a cost-effective basis.

GM's employee communication program was off and running under the public relations wing.

SHOULD OTHER STAFFS BE CONSIDERED?

While most of the discussion about location of the employee communication staff focuses on human resources and public relations, there are some who ask if it couldn't operate as well or better on other corporate staffs—or even be divided among two or more staffs.

An associate of mine said, "With the critical priority of product quality today, that's probably where at least a major thrust of our internal communication efforts should be—with the quality group." Another said, "Marketing has been directing mind-changing strategies in a highly-organized, scientific fashion for a long time. Maybe they could do a better job at influencing thinking and actions of our employees."

Injecting the advertising-marketing hype and mystique into the internal communication process would not be compatible with the kind of open, candid relationship that is essential for building durable credibility with a company's employee family.

There is also a trend toward considering employee communication as an integral part of an organization's strategic planning operation. In this scenario, special emphasis is placed on determining employee desires, as well as on stimulating more employee involvement in strategic planning and also making maximum use of the communication system in selling strategic plans to employees.

Employee communication is *not* the same as marketing, quality control, employee relations or strategic planning.

But there are dangers in many of these attempts to find a new, more productive home for the employee communication function. The truth, however, is that employee communication is not the same as marketing, quality control, employee relations or strategic planning. It's a professional specialty with its own unique characteristics, demands, technology, skills and professional standards.

Concentrating on just one key priority of an organization—like product quality or marketing—would quickly overload and overkill the employee communication system. That often happens with joint management-union publications, when so much emphasis is put on topics agreed to by both sides—so much so that a lot of controversial information important to both management and employees is played down or totally excluded.

Actually, one of the most credible elements of an effective employee communication process is the objective balance it provides to all major aspects of the business, including public relations.

Fragmented Approach Not Effective

Another important consideration is the critical need for coordinated, efficient management of an organization's total communication efforts, in which day-by-day activities are directed toward both a common long-range mission and strategic objectives. A fragmented approach rarely—if ever—can achieve the kind of consistent, cost-effective communication effort required in today's highly competitive environment.

Dr. James E. Grunig, of the University of Maryland, supports this viewpoint when he says that "excellent public relations organizations"—with responsibilities for both internal and external communication—will integrate all public relations functions into a single staff rather than subordinate them under other staffs such as personnel, marketing, or finance.

Only in an integrated department is it possible for public relations to be managed strategically.

When marketing practitioners manage public relations,...public relations is usually reduced to technique rather than strategy. Public relations practitioners are mere technicians working in support of marketing rather than public relations objectives.[3]

There are some communication professionals who say it doesn't matter where the function is located, as long as it is given proper recognition and support as part of the company's top management strategy. But most veteran practitioners believe that its location is a critical factor in determining how well and how professionally the function will be able to operate.

There is also compelling logic to have the activity report directly to the chief executive officer. This would provide the CEO with unscreened recommendations and counsel in this important area. It would avoid the inevitable politics and power tussles and officially give the function a higher position of prestige and authority than it enjoys in most companies today.

But at this point in time, it appears that most companies will continue to have employee communication functions operate at a secondary level, on either public relations or human relations staffs and, it is hoped, at least on a par with external communication.

PROS AND CONS: PERSONNEL AND PUBLIC RELATIONS

So, let's examine some of the basic considerations involved in deciding which of these two staffs is the most logical home for employee communication in a typical business firm.

In most organizations, the public relations staff is the established communication unit. It has professionals with the backgrounds and experience needed to fill employee communication positions, and it has the know-how to secure qualified professionals from outside the company if necessary.

In contrast, a personnel staff has to maintain parallel professional positions filled by people responsible to executives who, in most cases, have no training or experience in communication. Too often, persons assigned to the communication function on personnel

---

[3] James E. Grunig, ed., *Excellence in Public Relations and Communication Management: Contributions to Effective Organizations* (Hillsdale, N.J.: Lawrence Erlbaum Associates, forthcoming, 1991).

staffs end up being "available heads" who have little or no communication skills or professional commitment.

Consistency, Promptness, Regularity, Objectivity

The matter of consistency, promptness and regularity is critical to the credibility of the total corporate communication process. Public relations professionals are usually major architects in drafting the organization's communication messages. They are experienced in eliminating political problems early and in expediting approvals of news materials. They understand news values and deadlines; prompt action and regular communication are second nature to them.

The public relations staff has another important advantage when it comes to objectivity and the ability to maintain a balanced approach in internal news distribution. Because the personnel staff creates such a large volume of news concerning employees, it is difficult for its people—even those with the most honest intentions—to take a completely objective view in communicating these matters. On the other hand, the PR staff—if it does its job right—is responsible for seeing that all news stories originating within the company are written in a way which is in keeping with the corporate perspective.

As United Technologies' Ken Turpin says:

> Our ability to provide independent counsel would be compromised if we were part of another staff other than public relations. Although we work closely with other departments and staffs, we must be able to criticize when appropriate, and to elevate final decision making to higher levels when disagreements cannot be resolved at the staff level. If we were on some other staff, this type of objective evaluation and criticism would not be possible on activities for which that staff was responsible.

From the standpoint of working relationships, it is natural to expect frictions between news relations and employee communication functions.

Certainly the power and politics inherent in the access, control and distribution of information are factors which breed competition and turf tussles between these two functions. If the two communication activities are on separate staffs, the potential for turf, politics and power clashes is obviously much greater.

But there are also fundamental differences in goals. While both seek to distribute information which tells the facts as well as the company's viewpoint on news events, employee communication professionals have an obligation to tell more about the "hows" and "whys" which help to explain the impact of the news on employees, their work and personal security.

Career Pathing of Professionals

Another consideration is career pathing for communication professionals. It is much tougher for personnel staffs to hire and retain the better communicators. The potential for varied experience, increasing responsibilities and compensation in the communication field will, in most cases, be more favorable on public relations staffs. And chances of inter-staff promotions are unlikely.

There is one important final benefit to having internal communication as a function of the public relations or corporate communication staff. In working closely with other communication disciplines on the PR staff, employee communication managers have the opportunity to fight for and sell their viewpoint repeatedly as part of the overall public relations policy and practice. In this way, employee needs and concerns become a primary consideration in an organization's total communication process—external as well as internal. This is a highly desirable goal.

EXPERIENCES AT OTHER COMPANIES

General Electric. GE recently transferred its corporate employee communication function from industrial relations to public relations.

The main purpose of this change was to have all corporate communication professionals working off the same information base rather than to have two sources. According to Jim Harmon, formerly GE's manager of corporate employee communication and now program manager of personnel relations, the two-source method often leads to "chain losses" and misunderstandings. He continues:

> Under the old system, we had somewhat of a "Tinkers-to-Evers-to-Chance" distribution routine, and too often employee communication was the "Chance" in our communication chain. The new system at GE allows all communicators to receive the same information at the

same time from the same high source, from which point the professionals can act upon it and shape it for the different internal and external audiences. The flow of information is much smoother—no doubt about it.

But there is a possible downside. This stems from the fact that corporate employee communication professionals aren't official members of the personnel team—an out-of-sight, out-of-mind situation that could result in some bobbled balls. So, we have to work harder to stay close to the employee relations leaders and provide them with top-flight support.

So, the upside is that employee communication people in GE are now getting the information—our stock in trade—more directly and more quickly, bringing significant improvements in timeliness, content and consistency to the individual business unit communication functions. The possible downside is that the industrial relations people are further away from the communication function, and great care and effort must be expended to ensure that their communication needs are properly served.

ALCOA. The employee communication function was transferred back to corporate communications in early 1990 after six years as a responsibility of employee relations.

Bob Washburn, who continues as manager of the function, says the change was made to consolidate internal and external communication activities and to give more focus to ALCOA's total communications effort. But he emphasized that his department will retain a close working relationship with employee relations, symbolized by a dotted-line relationship to that staff.

> A lot of important news concerning employees originates on the employee relations staff at ALCOA. Because of my special involvement with that staff, I can participate in discussions and decisions concerning these matters—operating on the same level as managers of such key areas as employee health, safety, benefits, compensation and the sensitive area of labor relations.
>
> This means we can provide counsel on the communication aspects of personnel programs from the beginning rather than after the die is cast. In addition, our "insider" access to personnel information allows us to do a more effective job in overall communication planning.
>
> Employee communication will continue to be treated as part of the employee relations team rather than as an outsider. At the same time, our position on the corporate communications staff provides us with the opportunity to be a strong advocate for employee commun-

cation in helping to plan and execute the company's total communication strategy—and that should be a real plus.

Here are other viewpoints, representing both sides of the discussion:

Parker Hannifin. Communications vice president Dick Charlton emphasizes the importance his company places on putting all communication activities—external and internal—into one department.

> This allows Parker Hannifin to achieve maximum synergy and productivity by having all available human resources in this critical area rowing in the same boat. Having central direction also provides an important advantage in coordinating our total communication activities.

Atlantic Richfield. Dave Orman, manager of employee communications, works on the personnel staff and believes that's where his function belongs—at least at ARCO.

> Traditionally, when some management action had to be communicated, the first priorities were the public, or financial analysts, or shareholders. Employees were the last to know.
>
> But at ARCO, we don't have that problem. Our only priority is internal communication, and all of our efforts are focused on communicating with employees.
>
> We're able to overcome many of the problems public relations staffs have in communicating personnel issues and benefits—even the role of employee relations—by being one of them. We're not some stranger they don't know; we're part of their management team.
>
> If we have disagreements, they're with managers of areas like benefits or compensation, who are my peers and…have the same boss. So, we arbitrate the matter within our own staff rather than having two staffs which have to go to higher levels… which only exacerbates the problem.

SUMMARY

Where the employee communication function belongs continues to draw conflicting opinions, with one recent study showing a trend toward placing this responsibility in the human resources area but another showing a decided preference toward public relations. Generally speaking, it appears that in smaller companies, personnel is the preferred choice but the larger the organization, the more likely it is that the employee communication activity will be a part of the public relations staff.

Past performance of both personnel and public relations staffs leaves much to be desired in projecting which deserves future ownership. But the urgent need for professional, effective employee communication programs is going to impose higher standards of expectations for this function wherever it is located in the organizational hierarchy.

In theory and practice, the most cost-effective communication efforts are achieved when all communication functions are integrated on a single staff. Otherwise, successful strategic management is severely handicapped. Also, efficiency and cohesion are diluted.

Effective employee communication requires close cooperation between public relations and personnel people—and also with other key staffs, such as finance, marketing and legal. The personnel staff is a prime source of employee news and has the most to gain (or lose), depending on how effectively information is shared with employees. Also, in many companies, personnel people handle the internal communication function at the local levels.

Personnel staffs have much to gain from good employee communication—in terms of employee performance, loyalty and satisfaction. Working together, public relations and personnel people can help the internal communication function produce the greatest benefits for the organization and for all employees.

Case 10

New United Motor Manufacturing, Inc.

GENERAL MOTORS-TOYOTA JOINT VENTURE IS A MODEL OF MANAGEMENT-UNION-EMPLOYEE COOPERATION

General Motors and Toyota undertook a revolutionary project in 1983 when they agreed to a joint venture for assembling small cars in the former GM plant at Fremont, California, which had been permanently closed in 1982.

The project was designed to share experience and expertise in manufacturing, supplier relationships, union-management relations and the use of human resources.

Of special interest was the role of communication in achieving company goals, an effort which relies heavily on face-to-face communication on a regular, continuing basis. Such communication can serve as a strong thread to hold the fabric of participatory management together. The point is often made that much of the Japanese business success comes from outstanding communication systems which make every employee a communicator.

New United Motor Manufacturing, Inc. (NUMMI) was founded as an independent company with fifty-fifty ownership by Toyota and GM. Plans called for building up to 250,000 cars a year, with a staff of about 2,500 hourly and salaried employees.

NUMMI Objectives

The NUMMI experiment had the following objectives:

- For GM, it was a unique opportunity to gain first-hand experience with the efficient Toyota Production System (TPS), knowledge which could be shared with all GM operations. Also, it provided the opportunity to test Toyota principles in working with both employees and unions. Finally, GM would obtain a high-quality small car—the Nova—for its Chevrolet Division.

- For Toyota, it was an opportunity to gain experience with American unionized labor and suppliers, which could be used in expanding its manufacturing presence in the United States.

The project was launched from a rocky beach.

The Fremont plant, in its 20 years of operation as a GM facility, had a bad record of ugly, continuing management-labor confrontations which were costly in terms of quality, efficiency and morale. It had one of the worst disciplinary records in GM and, when it closed, had a backlog of more than 1,000 grievances and an absenteeism rate of over twenty percent. Management and the United Auto Workers (UAW) agreed that the majority of the NUMMI work force would come from laid-off employees, but extensive screening and assessment were used to select employees who could work with the new approach.

On the plus side, Toyota brought to the table a proven production system capable of turning out high-quality products on a very efficient basis and with strong employee participation. It also brought a reputation for outstanding human relations, one based on mutual trust and respect and open, two-way communication with its employees.

Top responsibility for running the NUMMI plant rests with Toyota executives—Kan Higashi is president and chief executive officer, and Osamu Kimura is executive vice president and chief operating officer.

TOYOTA PRODUCTION SYSTEM

The TPS relies heavily on the team approach and involves three basic concepts:

1. *Just-in-Time Production.* The goal is not to build cars for sale, but to replace those which are sold. This avoids waste of material, labor and facilities and of forcing unwanted products into the distribution system. Quality problems that otherwise would be hidden in excess inventory are spotlighted and solved rapidly, minimizing rework and waste.
2. *JIDOKA—The Quality Principle.* JIDOKA is a work philosophy which says quality should be assured in the production process itself instead of in the repair process, and every employee has the responsibility of either repairing defects on the line if possible, but if not, to stop the line until problems are resolved. The objectives are 100 percent quality, prevention of equipment breakdowns and efficient use of manpower.

3. *Full Use of Workers' Abilities.* Team members are treated with consideration, respect and as professionals; they are trained to be multi-functional and to contribute to decisions within their work group.

SUPERVISOR-EMPLOYEE ROLES REDEFINED

A very important part of the NUMMI system is the cooperative relationship which exists between management and the UAW, a relationship that was established with a new union contract containing many features considered revolutionary at that time.

Traditional class barriers and symbols were removed. All workers were to be treated as equals and were called "team members" rather than "employees." There were to be no time clocks and no special executive cafeterias or parking spaces.

An "open-office environment" had all management people, except for the president, sitting in open areas, dramatizing the easy access employees were to have to management.

Management roles were redefined. Hourly unionized employees— "team leaders"—supervised four-to-six workers. Traditional authoritarian first-level supervisors were replaced by group leaders, who worked for consensus actions and greater involvement by the twenty to twenty-five production-line workers they supervised. At least two layers of supervision which are present in typical assembly plants were eliminated.

Job classifications were reduced from more than 100 to only three— one covering all production jobs and two for skilled trades. These broader job classifications are essential for the Toyota Production System, in which team members are trained to do other jobs performed by the team.

The union contract guarantees strong job security. In the 1983–89 period, despite sharp dips in market demand, no employees were laid off. When line speeds are trimmed, affected employees are given other assignments or scheduled for extra training.

COMMUNICATION PLAYS IMPORTANT ROLE

Informed, understanding, participating employees are critical to NUMMI's success. But the communication process is far more than a weekly news summary, a bimonthly employee magazine, a weekly plant newsletter and departmental newsletters. The major share of communication is done face-to-face and by employee understanding gained through involvement in broad aspects of the operation.

The annual development of NUMMI goals and objectives is a prime example of how the system—and three-way communication—works through the organizational structure.

Executive officers each December develop a broad overview of the company's business picture and future events expected to affect operations. Functional objectives are developed by lower-level executives and their employees. Six key areas are included—quality, quantity, cost, human resources, communication and corporate citizenship. Each department develops its own goals and objectives; once approved by top management, they are discussed with all team members at a company-wide meeting in late January.

Throughout the year, objectives are checked for progress, and formal reviews occur in July and December.

The NUMMI decision-making process is based on consensus by all areas affected by decisions to be made. Minor decisions are pushed down to lower-levels so that only major and policy decisions are required of top management.

To support these processes—both in terms of annual goals or new activities—special emphasis is placed on the effective flow of information throughout the company. Various types of team and group meetings are held regularly to ensure two-way communication of established or emerging business issues.

WORKING AND SHARING TOGETHER

"The key for success in these procedures and the total NUMMI management process in general is an inherent feeling of working and sharing together," says Sharon Sarris, manager of community relations.

> The teamwork philosophy requires a healthy two-way exchange of information, problems and ideas from top to bottom and sideways. Essentially, everybody should know what's going on and how they fit in.

> The NUMMI philosophy takes the position that people want to be productive, and those closest to the operation understand best how to bring about improvements—and that's the focus of our face-to-face communication.

Training has ranked as a top priority from the beginning, when new employees were given hundreds of hours of classroom and on-the-job training. More than 450 team and group leaders participated in three weeks of classroom and on-the-job training at Toyota's Takaoka plant in Japan. Heavy emphasis on training continues, especially in problem solving, which is so fundamental to the team-concept system.

FIVE-YEAR PROGRESS

What were the results of the first five years of the NUMMI project? How successful was the Toyota Production System in converting a rebellious work force—by virtue of a totally different management style—into one which could compete against the world in producing small cars? Results for 1988 in four key areas provide some remarkable answers:

- *Product Quality.* NUMMI's Nova ranked second among 144 cars polled in the highly-respected J. D. Power Associates Customer Satisfaction Survey.

- *Attendance.* The figure for the Fremont plant was better than ninety-five percent, and this compared to about eighty-five to ninety percent for typical U.S. domestic assembly plants.

- *Grievances.* Fewer than sixty formal grievances were filed in 1988, and this compares to several hundred for typical U.S. domestic plants.

- *Employee Suggestions.* More than seventy percent of NUMMI's employees submitted at least one suggestion, and this compared to under ten percent for typical assembly plants.

Business Week says that GM and other U.S. auto makers have learned plenty from NUMMI. It adds that by 1996, when the current agreement between GM and Toyota on NUMMI expires, "...GM hopes to have absorbed NUMMI's chief benefit: the notion that better management, not massive automation, is the key to efficient manufacturing."[4]

---

[4] Robert D. Hof and James B. Treece, "Shaking Up Detroit," *Business Week* (August 14, 1989), p. 79.

Chapter 8

Obstacles to Good Communication: Nobody Promised You a Rose Garden

Change is never easy to sell. And when it involves major modifications in established communication concepts and systems, the combination of politics and information power can create serious obstacles.

Some occur more in central-office staffs; others are more obstructive at middle and lower levels of an organization. These obstacles can be found in all types of organizations—and often exist without being recognized as problems by top management. But all represent serious barriers to a free flow of information to and from employees throughout an organization.

Some communication managers are reluctant to talk about obstacles for publication, fearful that this might be embarrassing to them or their company's management. Others don't have problems because they are not aggressive in the intensity of their efforts for improvement. But privately, and at professional meetings, they open their frustration folio, seeking consolation or looking for solutions to thorny problems that thwart their efforts to achieve truly effective employee communication systems.

Let's examine eight major obstacles and discuss ways of defeating, or at least minimizing, their impact:

- Lack of management understanding and support.
- Autocratic rules of information sharing.
- Fear of the truth, of reporting bad news as well as the good.
- Non-communicator personnel types.
- Labor relations: behind closed doors.
- News relations: power of the press.
- Lack of adequate staff and budgets.
- The problem of recruiting and keeping top talent.

The first three obstacles deal with basic management philoso-phy—the most pervasive, insidious and often the most camouflaged obstructions to open communication. Few institutions or their top executives want to admit that as a matter of basic leadership performance, they don't believe in, or practice, good communication with their people.

Yet, here is what a survey of fifteen representative U.S. com-panies revealed. Eight companies said inadequate personnel and budgets were barriers. Seven cited autocratic rules of information sharing. Six companies listed lack of management understanding and support, fear of the truth, traditional personnel practices and labor relations as serious problems. Recruiting and keeping good people were listed by five companies. And four companies listed turf/power infighting with media relations as a problem.

MANAGEMENT UNDERSTANDING AND SUPPORT

Much has already been said about the frozen middle and higher levels of management which contribute to constipation of organiza-tional communication. Also discussed was the critical need for enlightened management, for executives who respect the need of employees to know what is going on and who understand the benefits that better informed, more understanding employees can bring to organizational performance.

When we talk about the need for top management understand-ing and support, we do not mean it is enough for executives to approve adequate personnel and budgets—or even for them to cooperate in reporting and approving top-level stories or other activities. It's a matter of total involvement. It calls for executives who recognize the tremendous potential of communication for helping them manage and produce better results.

Virtually all managers acknowledge the importance of good communication in carrying out their responsibilities. But many of them don't have the confidence in themselves to do it well, or they don't know how to engage in a participative, sharing way with their people. Or they simply don't understand how sophisticated and sensitive the employee communication function is in creating employee trust, confidence, commitment and job motivation.

Need Strong Commitment to Be Open and Honest

Most executives "talk a straight line," but the walking performance of many is wobbly if not halting.

The goal is not fancy rhetoric or surface support of major communication projects. Most executives "talk a straight line" when it comes to employee communication, but the walking performance of many is wobbly if not halting. What is sorely needed is a strong commitment to be open and honest with employees as much as possible and to demonstrate this commitment through actions, large and small, every day.

In some cases, this is a frustrating, discouraging assignment. One veteran communicator says about his company: "Our management professes support but favors upbeat, evasively-written articles. They are trying to delegate authority downward, but our centralized, authoritarian culture is hard to break down."

Brad Whitworth of Hewlett-Packard says:

> The number one problem for us is the laid-back attitude of many of our management people who believe that good, two-way communication just happens. Our general managers do a lot of "coffee-pot talks" and "management by walking around"; and some pretty much assume that gets the job done.

Another employee communication manager gives this straight-forward assessment of where his firm stands on information sharing with employees and what content his management prefers most:

> Generally, I'd say our management is more supportive than ever of "let's pat them on the back" employee recognition stories; of cliché-ridden articles about product quality, and of stories dealing with cost-cutting, employee safety, community affairs, management profiles and any subject that begins and ends on an upbeat note.
>
> Management needs to hear—from anyone who has the guts to stand up and tell them—that what employees want is plainly spoken, honest stories about the company's strategies and how employees fit in, along with information on career development and controversial issues that affect their employment.

GM Executives Confused Communication with Public Relations

Maryann Keller says that top General Motors executives in the 1980s failed to understand "the true meaning of communication in the corporation culture. ...They confused communication with public relations."[1]

I'm sure that's a common failing among the nation's top business executives, government leaders, university presidents and other high management officials from every type of large public and private institution.

But professional communicators must share the blame with managers who don't understand employee communication, who don't appreciate its full value in the management process and who don't apply sound communication principles in their own leadership roles.

Communicators Must Take the Initiative

On the positive side, Tom Martin of Federal Express believes that communicators must take the initiative in stimulating strong involvement of senior executives, not just during crises but on a continuing basis, and he works hard to achieve that goal. Martin

---

[1] From *Rude Awakening: The Rise, Fall and Struggle for Recovery of General Motors* by Maryann Keller. Copyright (c) 1989 by Maryann Keller. Reprinted by permission of William Morrow & Co.), p. 115.

says "the continuous touch of our top executives strengthens their understanding and support of the total communications effort." (For discussion of the total FedEx communication system, see Case Example 11 at the end of this chapter on pages 204-8.)

It's very easy to blame "the guys upstairs" or "the guy in the corner office." It is true that many executives don't understand the communication process and how it can work to their benefit. They like to deal with things they can control. The mercurial, sometimes explosive and always complex art of trying to win employee understanding by telling the whole truth can boggle the minds of traditional managers.

In most cases, however, managers don't get to the top by being stupid or by ignoring useful resources. But they are human. They have to deal with a lot of problems and challenges. They are buffeted by countless pressures to use this or that technique, idea or resource.

Communicators who are winners are the ones who sell their ideas best in an environment with that kind of competition. In some cases, the communication manager who wins is the one who has the guts to tell the CEO the truth—even though the boss may not want to hear it or believe it.

AUTOCRATIC RULES OF INFORMATION SHARING

Earlier, we made the point that, in the context of a modern management philosophy, authoritarian managers are an endangered species, costly relics which most organizations can no longer afford in today's highly competitive environment. We discussed the urgent need for broader employee participation in helping to achieve higher levels of performance and employee satisfaction in all kinds of organizations—public and private. And we emphasized the point that well-informed employees are critical to the achievement of these and other organizational goals.

Yet, a disturbing paradox persists in the way many organizations talk about communication with their employees—and what they actually do. While significant improvements have been made in American industry in recent years, the practice of honest, open sharing of information with employees is still a distant goal for many firms.

At the heart of the problem is a lack of trust on the part of management to share inside information with employees, even with managers, for fear it will be leaked to the news media or the competition. This is true even if top management has a good understanding of the potential of communication and what it can contribute to organizational goals. Also, many managers and organizations guard information jealously as a source of power, as an elitist perk reserved for higher-level managers only.

Accordingly, in most organizations, traditional autocratic rules of information sharing remain in effect—officially or unofficially—enforced by bureaucratic and cumbersome approval systems and restricted distribution policies. Too often, the "need to know" rule still applies.

Management Mistrusts Employees

Automotive analyst Maryann Keller criticizes business and General Motors for their negative attitudes toward employees and believes this is a definite factor in the decline of America's competitive strength.

> American companies tend, fundamentally, to mistrust workers. There is a pervading attitude that if you give them an inch, they'll take a mile, because they don't really want to work. ...More than anything else, GM's philosophy on people has contributed to its loss of the competitive edge. There is no trust. No respect.[2]

GM, too, recognized its relationship with employees as critical and has been devoting substantial efforts to regain the high levels of respect and loyalty it had traditionally enjoyed with employees. Strong management actions were symbolized by the issuance of a formal "People Philosophy" in 1988, whose theme was: "We value GM people above everything else."

The statement also says: "We will achieve success by providing our people with an environment which respects the dignity of every individual, which fosters trust in relationships and allows each person the opportunity to realize their full potential as individual and team members."

---

[2] From *Rude Awakening: The Rise, Fall and Struggle for Recovery of General Motors* by Maryann Keller. Copyright (c) 1989 by Maryann Keller. Reprinted by permission of William Morrow & Co.), pp. 124–25, 129.

Obviously, a "People Philosophy" is only a piece of paper unless management actions truly support it consistently and make it a way of life over time.

Lack of Trust Is Serious Obstacle

The condescending, distrustful manner which some operating managers—and staff people, too—adopt when dealing with employees *is* a serious obstacle. Some managers are reluctant to tell employees the whole truth because they feel "employees won't be able to understand; they don't know how to factor in the negatives or potential problems."

Some managers have been burned by poor communication or by good communication gone awry—and they "aren't going to try that again." And some don't trust employees with sensitive information because it might end up in the newspaper or on TV, or it might be passed along to competitors.

Many managers are unwilling to trust employees fully "until they have proven themselves." And once a trust has been violated, even by one employee, the information blackout is again in force. If managers really want an honest, open and trusting relationship with employees, they must go more than half way and do what is best for the majority of employees.

Some managers create their own bad dreams by not bringing employees on board as fully-informed, fully-participating members of the team. They look at information as a source of power which they are extremely reluctant to surrender even though it might contribute to increased performance.

Yet, the truth is that information is power only when it is put to use—and the wider its use, the more it generates changes in attitudes and actions which can be highly beneficial to the entire organization.

Some managers are also afraid they don't know how to share information properly so that it becomes a vital resource for increasing performance and trust. Rather, they act in fear of the possibility that information which leaks outside will boomerang and bring criticism from higher management. As a result, they share little or nothing and keep the lid tight on information which could be very useful to employees in doing their jobs at a high level of performance.

Approval Systems

Complex, powerful approval systems are one of the most obvious symptoms of an autocratic, distrustful communication process. They can be a nightmare for the conscientious communicator.

Ken Turpin, manager of employee communications at United Technologies, calls the approval system a major obstacle for his program.

> Since we are constantly pushing the limits of candidness in our communication efforts, we occasionally encounter executives who are reluctant to share all the information with employees. With top management support, however, we are winning a majority of the battles and convincing more and more executives that fuller sharing of information will pay off in increased employee trust, confidence in management and performance on the job.

Sandy MacKie, internal communications manager for Chevron Corporation, says that copy approvals, which represent his biggest obstacle, have a "negative impact on timeliness, cost-effectiveness, quality of writing and staff morale. All other problems in doing the employee communication job are minor compared to the clearance maze."

IBM's Les Simon says:

> Approval systems used to be cumbersome, with many people having to sign off before release. But our management recognizes that the world now is so fast-moving, that authority for approval has to be delegated to the operating level. The coming of internal TV makes this even more critical. You simply can't produce daily TV shows if the review process is cumbersome and bureaucratic.

The most hated two-word phrase among professional communicators is: "Kill it!" That's a typical response from non-communicators who object to an article for any number of reasons, but give comments like this: "I just don't like it. It's too sensitive. The chairman certainly won't like it. We've never talked about that before."

An employee communication manager should never kill any good story without a fight! If the story was worth doing to begin with, and the time has already been spent in researching and writing it, then it's worth saving. Reasonable objections can be accommodated while still retaining the basic thrust and meat of the story. But once executives (usually mid-level) are permitted to kill one or two stories with a blanket destruct, the credibility of the communication function is seriously bent.

The "Confidential" Stamp

Among the biggest problems communicators encounter are restrictions placed on many internal documents by the CONFIDENTIAL stamp. It seems like the confidential label is put on almost everything but the boss' Christmas card list. A lot of inside information is tightly guarded as a source of power—to be used or withheld for personal or political gains—and where this is a regular procedure, the internal communication system suffers accordingly.

The truth is that employees really aren't interested in a lot of technical and financial details that are usually the truly proprietary part of "inside information." Their needs are much more general: They want to know what's happening in the business, where it's heading and how it affects them. And answering those questions in general terms usually doesn't involve any deep, dark secrets. There's no need to quarantine the whole town to keep one family under cover.

It's important to simplify the approval system as much as possible—the fewer reviewers the better. It's best to have a core of regular reviewers in key areas such as public relations, personnel, finance and legal, whom you can educate about your mission and goals and with whom you can develop a partnership. If assigned a reviewer who won't let you do your job in a professional and honest manner, find some way to get a replacement.

"Advance concept" approvals of publication articles or other new communication projects by an advisory committee of top executives can help to eliminate a lot of objections and attempted censorship at final review time.

As a practical matter, approvals should be fairly simple as long as the copy is accurate and of good quality in content and writing skill—and as long as key management people understand and support your basic communication goals.

FEAR OF TELLING THE TRUTH

There is a strong tendency among management executives to distribute rose colored glasses along with company news releases, even when talking to employees. "Why discuss the negative aspects? The media and critics always do a good job in this respect."

Many executives also believe that employees can't handle negative news; that they don't have the background or abilities to balance the pluses and minuses and arrive at the truth. Others are paranoid on the subject and believe employees can't be trusted with inside information, particularly bad news, and that they will feed it to the competition or to the news media.

Excuses for Not Communicating Honestly

These are ridiculous excuses for not communicating honestly with employees.

In the first place, today's employees are very knowledgeable and sophisticated; their access to business information is not restricted to the company newsletter but can come from an amazing variety of print, audio and visual media. Secondly, employees have a personal stake in the welfare of the company rivaling that of top executives—even if the monetary levels are different—and they need to be well-informed in order to be fully-participating team members. Finally, it is rare when bad news doesn't end up in the news media quickly anyway, regardless of internal restrictions. If the company has been honest in telling employees first, the news will get a lot more balanced interpretation not only among employees but also among everyone they come into contact with.

PUTTING INFORMATION TO WORK

Those who jealously protect their information chests should remember that knowledge achieves maximum power when it is shared with people who can put it to work to make things happen. And the wider its use, the more powerful its charge. However, for those managers who grew up with stringent restrictions on information sharing, it's hard to accept a new philosophy that says they should share with employees all information that is not clearly detrimental to the organization.

In working situations today, more companies are sharing information formerly classified as confidential, including such data as quality defects, competitive comparisons on quality and costs, absenteeism, scrap rates, new product designs and manufacturing costs for components. And some of this internal information does occasionally end up in local newspapers or on TV.

But retired Chevron Chemical president Bob Davis warns that failure to share business information can be worse than having some facts leak to the competition.

> Some people say that if you talk to too many people about your strategy and plans, the competition is going to find out. But I'd rather have competitors know some things about us than have our own people in the dark about what we're trying to achieve. Communicating goals is crucial, because it's our employees who play perhaps the most important role in developing strategies designed to achieve those goals.[3]

Information-Sharing Feeds Continuous Improvements

Employees need a steady diet of business information so they can understand how they are doing on their jobs and how they compare with other plants in areas like quality. It also helps them to understand how their work compares with the competition, and what it takes to ensure their own personal security. It's the free flow of ideas which produces the improvement so badly needed for success.

As Tom Peters says in *Thriving on Chaos:*

> The reality is that millions—literally an unlimited number—of innovation/improvement opportunities lie within any factory, distribution center, store or operations center. ...
>
> Only when we come to understand that the ideas are principally on the front-line (or in the supplier's operation), not in R&D or "higher up," will the fear of disruption recede. ...[Then] we will begin to search for ways to give workers more time to work at innovation, rather than threatening them at every turn.[4]

EMPLOYEE PARTICIPATION IS THE KEY GOAL

The drive for continuous improvement is why employee suggestions and strong face-to-face information sharing get special attention at the GM-Toyota plant in Fremont, California. In its suggestion plan,

[3] The employee publication of Chevron Corporation, *Chevron Focus* (August–September 1989), pp. 13–14.

[4] Tom Peters, *Thriving on Chaos* (New York, Random House, 1987), p. 267.

NUMMI emphasizes broad employee participation, an effort which promotes many small ideas rather than million-dollar ideas from a few employees. In 1988, more than seventy percent of NUMMI employees submitted suggestions; this figure compared to less than ten percent for a typical U.S. domestic auto assembly plant.

Ford Strengthens Communication Effort

Increased employee participation in the business was also a major reason behind substantial recent improvements in employee communication by Ford Motor Company.

Ford strengthened its internal communication effort following severe financial losses in the early 1980s and as part of major long-term changes in the way the company ran its operations. In 1988, Chairman Don Petersen told an internal conference of 400 company communicators:

> We came to realize during those trying times of the early '80s that the support of all our people was critical to achieving our future goals. We knew that, in the end, the success of our strategies for survival and our transformation around the globe depended almost entirely on the cooperation of the people who had to implement those strategies...that no matter how sound our business plans, this company could not move forward unless employees agreed to help—and did so willingly—indeed, enthusiastically.[5]

MANY FIRMS HAVE IMPROVED COMMUNICATION, BUT...

Beyond job-related information, many companies are making sincere efforts to communicate candidly with employees on the events, developments and plans affecting their jobs. Many firms also are sharing information in a major way regarding business matters and public issues facing corporate management.

Allstate's employee communication program, for example, devotes special attention to proposed government regulations affecting the insurance business. Dick Madden says:

> Certainly we need well-informed management people who can be official spokespersons for Allstate. But it is also important to em-

[5] Comments delivered by Donald Petersen, former Chairman of the Ford Motor Company, in a January 16, 1987 speech to the Foundation for American Communications, Naples, Florida.

power all employees with the facts so they can intelligently discuss Allstate issues at parties, neighborhood barbecues and in other community activities.

Good examples are the California referendum rolling back car insurance premiums and Allstate's decision to withdraw completely from the Massachusetts property and casualty insurance market because of restrictive regulations.

In too many places, the old rules, the old fears, the lack of trust and use of information as power still persist.

Unfortunately in too many places, the old rules, the old fears, the lack of trust and the use of information as power still persist— particularly among old-line managers still in key positions.

Employees are expected to know about the company's strategic plan, but it's like "pulling eye teeth" to get approvals to distribute such information beyond the very top layers of executives. Employees are expected to know why the company has to reduce employment and cut costs, but there is trauma if some part of this story leaks to the news media.

Let me make one point clear. Professional communicators in business concerns are not Robin Hoods or investigative reporters. They are paid to make their companies look as good as possible, without being untrustworthy or dishonest.

Organizational communicators are paid to perform informational activities which enhance the reputation and image of the company and which encourage management actions that contribute to open and honest communication with employees. This does not require unnecessary communication of negative information or rumors. Nor does it mean communicators have to give away proprietary information which could be damaging to the best interests of the company, its management or its employees. But it does suggest that presenting employees with both sides of controversies of major interest is not only the fair thing to do but also increases management's credibility with employees.

The communicator's job is to be aggressive and imaginative enough to present his or her company in a favorable light. This is done by emphasizing the positives and spotlighting company pluses to balance the normal negatives, errors or incomplete reporting of the mass media. When the media coverage turns up positive too, the employee communication inputs are all gravy.

Politics, Power and Turf Struggles Hurt Progress

Now, let's discuss some inherent problems faced by employee communication functions in dealing with other staff activities—specifically personnel, labor relations and news relations.

In these relationships, there are strong political forces at work, along with turf and power struggles. Control of information-distributing channels opens important avenues of power for accomplishment and recognition—for groups and individuals alike. The more effective the communication function, the greater its power. Real power brokers at staff levels usually have short-term selfish goals, but the long-range damage they can do to inter-staff teamwork can be devastating.

James E. Grunig of the University of Maryland says that in his research of companies with outstanding leadership, the "excellent leaders give people power, but minimize 'power politics.'" [6]

Let's examine each of these inter-staff relationships in sharper focus.

NON-COMMUNICATOR PERSONNEL EXECUTIVES

Personnel people, of course, have much to gain from good communication, especially in terms of getting employees to understand and appreciate personnel policies, actions and benefits. Positive attitudes about the company and good employee morale are prime objectives of personnel staffs—and effective communication can make major contributions to these goals.

In many companies, personnel executives understand the need for on-going, two-way communication as a means of developing feelings of sharing, teamwork and belonging. But some personnel people, particularly those who have been around for a while, are actually non-communicators by training and tradition, and in the basic mind-set which influences their day-to-day actions.

---

[6]James E. Grunig, ed., *Excellence in Public Relations and Communication Management: Contributions to Effective Organizations* (Hillsdale, N.J.: Lawrence Erlbaum Associates, forthcoming, 1991).

Their logic runs something like this: "Tell employees as little as possible. Restrict distribution to the smallest group necessary. Avoid bad news if possible. Why do we want to bring up that subject again? It'll just stir up problems where there aren't any."

Some personnel people also cling to their longstanding love affair with the caste system, which tends to restrict information sharing on important information as tightly—and as high up—as possible. They seem to find safe ground in highly technical, legal language which is difficult for employees to understand. There is also a tendency to avoid or obfuscate negative aspects with "rose-colored" prose, to show company policies in the best possible light—sometimes in a way which borders on lying.

One of the fundamental problems is that many personnel people—at top executive levels and down the line—do not understand the tremendous potential of effective communication: It can help them to get their personnel jobs done while allowing them to retain a favorable image and credibility with employees. But this failing certainly is not limited to personnel executives either.

As GM's Jack McNulty says about managers in general: "Another generation of managers probably has to fade out before the philosophy of open communication will be broadly accepted at every level of the organization."

And I'm sure that's true of many established institutions in America today, particularly those undergoing substantial changes in management styles and work environments.

There are encouraging signs, however, that a new breed of personnel professional is emerging, one with a strong recognition of the potential of good communication in helping to achieve personnel goals.

LABOR RELATIONS: BEHIND CLOSED DOORS

Labor relations poses a different but very formidable obstacle to open, honest communication with employees.

Some labor relations experts seem to believe that the unions have the prime responsibility for communicating with their members, particularly in problem areas. As a result, they seem to prefer that management stay on the sidelines, communicating little or no information of substance to unionized employees. This makes it difficult to incorporate in on-going communication plans, subjects which may be crucial to the next negotiations.

One high labor relations executive pooh-poohed my belief that better-informed union employees would be more likely to support management's position on contract negotiations—that is, support a reasonable contract if they had the facts. He said:

> The hard facts of reality are that union contracts are decided at the ballot box, and because of the usually poor turnout, the union leadership can control the elections. It doesn't matter how much employees know about the business if they don't vote.

That may be accurate—but if so, it is as damning an indictment of company union elections as it is of elections in the outside political arena.

Eleventh-Hour Blitzes Are the Normal Pattern

Traditionally, many labor relations people don't get very excited about communicating with union employees until 3 or 4 months before the start of new contract negotiations. Then, they're looking to mount an eleventh-hour blitz of external publicity, relying on a big play in executive speeches and a whirlwind series of visits by top executives to company operations which could influence contract ratification.

Communication of this type, done only at crisis time, is very transparent to employees and has little or no credibility. It's a waste of time and money that usually backfires, resulting in negative, rather than positive, reactions by employees.

As discussed before, the most effective communication plan when preparing for labor negotiations is one which involves a continuing, year-round program of information sharing whose major emphasis is on the areas likely to be the main union targets. With such a sound base of information about the business and its trouble spots, employees are much better prepared to understand both management and union positions.

Some employee communication managers seeking to carry on a continuing dialogue with employees about key business challenges have difficulty getting cooperation from labor relations people until crash time. Mostly, the process relies largely on secret discussions between union representatives and company negotiators. Often, it's a closed shop, and employee communication people are on the outside—just as the employees are.

Management-Union-Employee Communication

There are obvious reasons for closed-door sessions between company negotiators and union officials in the actual period of contract negotiations. It's understandable why neither side wants newspaper or TV hoopla disrupting what should be calm and reasoned discussion of critical issues.

But for the other ninety percent of the time, management should never surrender its right—and obligation—to communicate fully with its employees about the challenges facing the business. Any time these rights are violated, it has a detrimental effect on management's credibility.

A special program for communicating with the unions at the leadership level and targeting special information to unionized employees could produce real benefits all around, and some companies have done it successfully. But many find that the intense environment of politics and power and the manipulative use of information by both sides make it difficult, if not impossible, to integrate the communication goals of labor relations into long-range communication planning.

It's almost as though the unions and labor relations people want to keep the love-hate, running-confrontation relationship going to protect both their own power bases and reasons for existing. Unfortunately, the result is conflict and confusion as employees try to figure out who are the good guys and who are the bad. Or is it both? The constant bickering and anti-management charges by union leaders tend to corrode employee confidence and trust—not only in management but in union leadership as well.

In-Fighting Impedes Efforts to Survive

GM's Bob Stramy says that despite the competitive crisis confronting American industry, in-fighting among members of the industrial team severely impedes what should be mutual efforts to survive.

To our detriment, American industry is to this day characterized by adversarial relations between union and management, between worker and supervisor, and within the management ranks, and by a salaried and hourly work force whose goals and loyalties are not consistent with those of the organization.[7]

To summarize: the new spirit of "jointness" being emphasized by unions and management at many companies has the potential for bringing management, unions and all employees into more participative, contributory relationships. And most industry observers say this "maturity" is a welcome and long-overdue development.

However, these efforts tend to be fragile and volatile, depending on the interactions of personalities, politics and power by both management and union leadership. Current readings certainly do not signal a strong forecast of fair weather ahead in this traditionally combative and disruptive relationship.

MEDIA RELATIONS: POWER OF THE PRESS

Now, let's turn to the relationship between media relations and employee communication functions.

In more benevolent days, external news media coverage provided a planned communication channel for company news of interest to employees. In the past decade or two, however, the news media have become much more penetrating in their coverage of key issues of business, with increased emphasis on negative, sensational aspects.

The result has been to strengthen the quality and power of media relations functions in corporations. At the same time, these and other trends emphasized the critical importance of communicating to employees the company's positions on a variety of subjects, some of which are largely ignored or are unfairly interpreted by the mass media.

There are fundamental differences in the operations of typical news relations and employee communication functions—differences more pronounced in larger organizations.

Parker Hannifin's Dick Charlton points out:

> In the last two decades, most companies have put the greatest emphasis on communicating with customers and shareholders. In the '90s, while we can't neglect those external audiences, we're going to have to do a much more forceful job of internal communication. Motivating and retaining employees is essential to our success.

[7]Robert J. Stramy, John J. Nora and C. Raymond Rogers, *Transforming the Work Place* (Princeton, N.J.: Princeton Research Institute, 1986), p. 6.

Differences in Audiences

In comparing internal and external communication, we find that the audiences are significantly different in the types of information they want and need. Employees are part of the "family" looking for balanced reporting: "Don't just tell us the good stuff; we usually already know that. Tell us the bad news, too, and let us know how the good news/bad news affects us." The outside media more often than not are looking for the negative aspects which they will highlight, even if the positive aspects are included in the stories.

The basic nature of news relations departments is shaped by heavy demands from the external media. As a result, a large share of their efforts are reactive and defensive.

Emphasis on Long-Range Proactive Actions

Employee communication staffs, on the other hand, are better able to chart their own priorities and follow a more proactive, planned approach. More time can (or should) be spent in trying to answer the questions of "Why?" and "What does it mean to employees?"

This approach to employee communication places special emphasis on longer-range planning, trends, backgrounders and executive interviews that discuss the pros and cons of key issues. Good employee communicators solicit employee opinions about what's hot and what's not with respect to information. The goal is to give employees more than the "blue-plate special."

Media relations people often consider themselves to be the guardians of corporate information jewels. In some cases, important news of direct concern to employees—such as the closing of plants—gets to the launching pad without the counsel of employee communication experts. The opportunities for bad judgments, to give news media concerns precedence over employee interests, is obvious in such situations.

Employee communication professionals need to be in on the takeoff of critical flights—not just at the crash landings.

Greater Attention to Employee Interests

Only a few years ago, employees heard about most events—even those involving their own plants—through local newspapers or on radio and TV newscasts. Many companies have learned hard, bitter lessons from situations like this.

As a result, employee interests and concerns are now being given greater consideration. First release of employee-related news to employees is now standard procedure in many companies—most of the time.

In late 1989, for example, General Motors public relations came in for media criticism because it bypassed the normal channels for reporting company news. Instead of providing the usual corporate summary on changes in production shifts at a number of plants, it let each plant announce the changes to its own employees. After the media requested more information, it released news of the changes through group news relations staffs rather than from corporate sources. Because of the new procedure, the external news media had to collect the information from several affected groups, and that required more time. It also involved more work for GM group PR offices.

The significance of this new procedure was emphasized by Jack McNulty, formerly GM's vice president of public relations:

> It came about because of the recent emphasis on decentralization and on a more open, caring, and participative relationship with our employees. ...
> Our first obligation was to report the production shifts to the employees who would be involved. They clearly should hear it first and hear it from their local supervision.
> In earlier days, we would have been inclined to say "nothing to nobody," not until every "i" was dotted and every "t" was crossed. Now we tell the affected employees all that we know for sure (about production changes), even though there are many uncertainties still in the picture. The old way would have been neat, simple...and wrong.

Tough Competing with External Media

But it must be recognized that the external media employ 24-hour, heavy-hitting resources against which the internal communication function has to compete in getting priority company information to employees.

The power of the press works inside a company as well as outside, and so the communication function offers an enticing target of the politics-and-turf variety. Power politics and turf jealousies unfortunately are realities in any dynamic organization—and those who direct employee communication programs have to learn how to "swim with the sharks without being eaten alive."

Competition can be healthy. However, constant confrontation in any part of the corporate family—and that includes the unions—is disruptive and divisive, and it leads to waste. This competitive energy can be more wisely channeled into making a company more effective against outside competitors.

LESS IN-FIGHTING AND MORE COOPERATION IS NEEDED

Recent experience indicates there is increasing cooperation among these key staffs in major companies, particularly the public relations, personnel and labor relations staffs—and between internal and external communication sections.

Tom Martin of Federal Express believes communication professionals should get into more main-track activities of their organizations.

> Communication professionals need to be more aggressive in getting into the game, becoming part of the overall strategic planning process at their companies. This means getting well educated on business issues and staying closely connected in meaningful ways to such key staff areas as personnel, legal, finance and marketing.

All in all, it is simple logic that the employee communication function can achieve its maximum effectiveness by working in close sync—as a peer—with other key management activities. Links to media relations, personnel, labor relations, strategic planning, quality and marketing are all highly important—although it's always comforting to have the legal and financial staffs in your corner, too.

But communication managers must beware of "helping hands" that seek not to advise but to control.

It is critical, however, that these key staffs develop a common bond of understanding and cooperation. Joint research involving a company's total communication activities can help define responsibilities for internal and external communication—as well as the role other staffs could play in the total process. The communication professional should take the initiative in seeking strong inter-staff relationships—in organizing a unified attack using the tremendous potential of employee communication to achieve the most good for everyone.

At the beginning of this chapter, I listed two additional obstacles to good communication:

1. The lack of adequate staff and budget, and
2. The problem of recruiting and keeping good talent in the employee communication function.

These problems are much less severe than they were 10 or even 5 years ago. But they still represent serious problems for employee communication managers in many companies.

SECURING ADEQUATE STAFF AND BUDGET

Realistically, few professionals get all the people and money they feel they need to conduct a top-notch employee communication program. This is particularly true of nonprofit organizations and especially those involved with social, health and community services.

With these organizations, limited funds are an accepted fact of life. Because of this, employee communication has a special appeal for them; it can motivate employees to be as productive as possible and to find maximum gratification from the type of work they do. It also places a premium on employee enthusiasm and loyalty in their contacts with the outside public, the group from which these organizations must gain their on-going support.

As recently as 10 years ago, many companies did little or nothing to communicate in a professional way with employees. Ditto for nonprofit organizations. As a result, building adequate staffs and budgets from scratch has been tougher for this field than for other established functions like media relations, advertising or stockholder relations.

Fortunately, things have changed for the better. As the caliber of people in this field has improved, so has the recognition of the value of the function—with more staff and bigger budgets coming as a natural consequence. But improvements have not been good enough yet, not by any stretch of the imagination. And future gains will continue to be tough because of the tighter economic controls brought on by increasingly intense worldwide competition.

So, what can employee communication departments do to help ensure proper manpower and budgets?

As simplistic as it seems, the best strategy is to try and persuade management that the function *can* favorably influence bottom-line results. Good salesmanship, working in tandem with top performance, can help to ensure that final results match expectations and specific goals.

Performance and Salesmanship

The need for aggressive, opportunistic salesmanship cannot be overemphasized. Do a good job, and make sure the key people know the facts about what was accomplished and what is needed to make even greater contributions.

Keep in mind that communication programs should be strongly oriented toward company goals if they are to elicit strong management support. And communication managers should be tough judges of their own programs relying on regular testing with both informal and formal research. Proposals for new activities need thorough research, including studies of similar activities at other companies. Finally, in progress reports to management, special emphasis should be placed on how the communication program is helping to achieve company goals and on the fact that it is regularly evaluated and improved on a professional basis.

In starting a new communication program, the staff and its activities should be constructed like a house—one brick at a time. Don't try to construct the entire building all at once, only to find that you have too many of the wrong kinds of people for the kind of program which has developed. One or two fundamental activities need to be put into place—operating well and tested for effectiveness before expanding to other activities.

Study, plan, implement and test; study, plan, implement and test. Be patient.

It is highly important that employee communication managers be as tough in efficiency as they are demanding in effectiveness or editorial content. Being a good manager of all resources—including creative people—is just as important as being a good communicator.

Madison Avenue designs, six-color printing and luxurious paper stock aren't required to deliver effective messages. Content, clarity, timeliness and credibility are the critical elements—not glitter and gloss.

Creative Accounting

Creative accounting can be very helpful in demonstrating favorable cost-benefit ratios for top management. A line item of $1 million or more for an employee communication budget can present a juicy target for cost cutters, even though it may be a minimum-level budget. Translating it into annual costs per employee can present a remarkably different impression and also one more fair in terms of total impact on the business.

If you believe your company is behind comparable organizations in expenditures for employee communication, you may want to do a confidential survey to see exactly how you rate in both people and dollars.

GM did this in 1979 and 1982 in cooperation with a handful of well-known companies—including IBM, Du Pont, Xerox and General Electric—and the results were impressive. GM's personnel and activity costs per 50,000 employees were less than one-fifth of the average costs for the other companies. In fact, GM's program costs in 1982 were about ninety cents per employee, and this compared to the $4.85 average for the other companies, which ranged from $1.63 to $10 per employee.

The 1982 study was part of a corporate improvement effort which resulted in a significant expansion of both personnel and budgets for the corporate-level employee communication programs—and it was used by aggressive local communicators for selling expansion of their activities, too. The study provided convincing evidence in a language management understands and responds to.

Even if you decide only to calculate your *own* annual costs per employee—or per impressions—such data can provide a much more favorable cost/value relationship for your program.

Managing Creative People

Managing creative people to achieve both quality and productivity goals is also essential. Just because they have special talents doesn't mean they can set their own levels of performance, substance or expenditures. Reorganizing the communication function itself, changing reporting relationships and responsibilities to better fit the available talents and desires of people is another way of achieving better results in effectiveness, efficiency and morale.

Periodically, look for outmoded activities that can be junked, part time jobs that can be combined, or ways to streamline operations. Certainly, personal computers have revolutionized writing, secretarial work, printing and other traditional functions of communication departments; and good managers will take full advantage of these fabulous tools. Supplying personal computers for use at home can also increase productivity while giving writers greater flexibility about when and how to put in those extra hours so often required.

Don't ever give bean counters a target; be your own efficiency expert!

Don't ever give the bean counters a target when cost-cutting hatchets start chopping away. Be your own efficiency expert! If you are, management will be more likely to give your requests for additional people and funds positive consideration.

HIRING AND KEEPING GOOD TALENT

Recruiting and keeping top talent is another serious problem. This is complicated by the fact that at many companies, jobs in employee communication are of lower status and offer less potential for advancement and financial reward than those in media relations.

We discussed earlier the importance of a good educational background (heavy liberal arts and journalism, plus courses in behavioral psychology, business and government), plus hard writing experience. Look for candidates who show initiative, imagination and a touch of irreverence for the status quo. The organizational communication field certainly is exciting and challenging enough, if the process is a dynamic and integral part of an organization's total communication effort. So, hiring able people should not be difficult. Keeping them will probably be a more severe test.

In discussing the problem of keeping good people, AT&T's Ray O'Connell says:

Good people in employee communication tend to be promoted to other public relations assignments quickly. Many employee communication jobs—particularly publication writers and editors—are entry-level jobs and turnover is high. We have to admit that it's a great training ground that has helped strengthen our total public relations effort.

This kind of practice certainly doesn't encourage PR professionals who work in other areas to seek jobs in the employee communication section. And it does nothing for the strength and stability of employee communication either.

Also, once top people are recruited and show their stuff, because of the limitations on status and financial rewards, they become prime candidates for jobs elsewhere in the broader public relations or personnel fields. This compounds the problem of building and maintaining a capable staff and of getting the important employee communication job done right.

Pay and Career Planning Are Important

However, recruiting good people and training them for other public relations jobs do make a contribution to the company's total communication effort. And even though these people move on to other parts of the PR activity, it is hoped they will retain their understanding and support of the internal communication function.

The opportunity for employees to advance to higher-level responsibilities in other public relations posts should be a fundamental part of career planning. It is important that the employee communication department not be viewed as "a dead-end street" for employees who can't be placed elsewhere.

Preventing stagnation is also highly desirable. The ideal situation is to have regular cross-transfers with other corporate communication functions to provide varied experience and also an element of competition outside of your own backyard.

Good pay and other forms of recognition, of course, are extremely important for hiring and keeping good people. The employee communication manager must be aggressive in pushing for salary levels equal to those in other public relations functions, such as news relations, stockholder relations and financial reporting. Convincing evidence can be presented to prove that creativity, skills and intelligent strategic planning and management are just as critical in this field—if not more so—than in other aspects of corporate communication.

Memberships and active participation in professional organizations are also keys to full development as professionals. Most important of all is recognition for a job well done—in terms of running compliments, encouragement, promotions and salary increases.

Create Environment for Creative Thinking

One of the biggest and most exciting challenges for the manager of creative people is the development of an environment that nurtures, stimulates and rewards imaginative thinking. With creative people particularly, he or she who manages least manages best.

Creative people like to develop and carry out their own new ideas. This provides excellent experience and helps fuel enthusiasm and more ideas from other members of the staff.

Managers should be there to encourage free-thinking, to help make problem solving easier, to be facilitators and to support their people and their ideas. The goal should be to create an open, nonthreatening environment where rules are kept to a minimum, well-thought-out risk taking is encouraged and successful creativity is properly rewarded.

Again, the ability to hire and keep good people is improving as the importance of employee communication increases and the overall caliber of professionalism in this field continues to advance.

LESSONS LEARNED ABOUT MINIMIZING OBSTACLES

What are the lessons to be learned from experiences discussed in this chapter? Here are some ways to take a proactive approach to eliminate or minimize obstacles and build greater support.

- Make sure you have a solid base of understanding and support from your company's top executives—reinforced regularly with presentations and reports. A lot of lower-level obstacles can be eliminated or bypassed with on-going support from on high.
- Involve and communicate with top management at divisional and plant levels, too. Grass-roots advice and support can make the corporate effort more productive and more relevant to bottom-line results.

- Always have a short- and long-term plan for the employee communication program. This proactive approach will give your activity strength in the minds of management.
- Employee communication managers must be as tough in efficiency as they are demanding in editorial content. Being a good manager of all resources—including creative people—is just as important as being a good communicator.
- The organizational communicator must take the initiative in seeking the understanding of and cooperation from other key disciplines in the company—to seek strength through unity.
- Oppose the idea that unions should be the primary communication source for unionized employees concerning news of the business—good and bad. To do otherwise can seriously damage the prestige and credibility of the entire communication program and also impair management's ability to communicate freely with its employees.
- Don't ever give up on a good idea. Fall back, regroup and make another charge, maybe up the other side of the mountain. If it's a really good idea and you have the determination to win, you can make it come alive.

SUMMARY

Like a freshman pushing hard for a place on the varsity squad, employee communication in many companies is still fighting for proper recognition at the management table.

Change almost always breeds obstacles because of the established management environment, or because of procedures and organizational inertia—plus a strong human reluctance to change.

To overcome barriers to good communication, the best defense is a good offense. The employee communication manager must be aggressive in building a program based on sound management principles, one strongly oriented toward organizational goals and supported by solid evaluation. Special efforts should be directed to winning the understanding of and support from top management and also other key management disciplines. Target those in the human resources areas particularly, for whom employee communication offers special value as a resource.

Good solid results over time will blow away most obstacles for enlightened management.

CASE 11
Federal Express Corporation

MASSIVE COMMUNICATION SYSTEM COMBINING VIDEO AND PRINT

Top executives at Federal Express say their company is what it is today to a significant degree because of a strong employee communication program. And their actions speak even louder than their words.

FedEx has one of the most extensive, multi-dimensional employee communication programs anywhere in the world. It employs more than sixty-five professionals and has an annual budget of more than $8 million.

The FedEx employee communication staff showed its skills in helping to effect a smooth transition when the Flying Tigers organization was acquired in 1989. Prior to the acquisition, Flying Tigers was the world's largest air cargo airline, operating primarily overseas.

COMMUNICATION IS INTEGRAL PART OF DOING BUSINESS

The employee communication department annually produces more than 300 publication issues a year, including separate versions for management and several targeted employee audiences. Annual production over the FXTV satellite network involves more than 300 live broadcasts to more than 1,000 locations in North America, along with 100 videotaped programs to targeted audiences. The FXTV network has two-way audio capabilities at all North American locations.

Tom Martin, managing director of employee communications, is not modest about the magnitude of the system because he views it as an integral part of doing business in a highly competitive environment.

Federal Express has more than 85,000 employees around the world. Founded in 1973, its annual revenues have grown to more than $7 billion.

Here's how the company's top executives view the employee communication activity:

Fred Smith, chairman and CEO:
Our communication system is strongly oriented to the business side, and video particularly has demonstrated results to prove its value. It has contributed to improved customer services and employee attitudes, just to name two specific examples. FXTV allows us to give our employees a daily snapshot of our integrated delivery system every single morning. It also allows us to communicate priority news, such as our acquisition of the Flying Tigers organization almost immediately—and before they see it on external news channels. That means a lot to our employees.

Jim Barksdale, executive vice-president and chief operating officer:
We wouldn't be anywhere near the size we are, or as profitable as we are, or have such good relationships with our employees if we weren't deeply into the business of communicating with our people. There simply is no available alternative for not communicating with your employees to the best of your ability. It is critical that we communicate what the company is, its products, its mission and how to go about accomplishing our tasks. Anything less than 100 percent effort in communicating these kinds of information to your employees is a dereliction of management's duty.

SATELLITE TELEVISION NETWORK

The Federal Express satellite television network—FXTV—is impressive.

Daily satellite telecasts put on the air about 6:30 a.m. every morning (Memphis time) run 5–7 minutes; these are taped and then replayed all day at more than 1,000 North American locations. The system is being expanded to the United Kingdom and part of Europe and later, to the rest of continental Europe and Asia. Subjects include breaking news about the company and industry, stock prices, weather, safety tips, articles about employees and on-site reports of field operations.

Another fifty to sixty FedEx telecasts each year run 30–60 minutes as follows:

1. About twenty-five telecasts a year for the management group deal with personnel and policy issues, cost-reduction, and problem resolution for field operations and services. A "Leadership Series" of broadcasts covers examples of good management in such areas as communication, disciplinary problems, leadership and career development.

2. Another twenty-five telecasts a year are sales oriented, focusing on such subjects as new products, product services, selling strategies, and marketing and competitive trends.

3.   An additional ten to twelve telecasts a year are directed to all employees on such subjects as pay and benefits, global business, improving paperwork accuracy and competition.

SIXTY INTERACTIVE SHOWS A YEAR

About sixty programs a year are interactive—with two-way audio transmissions via an 800 number, available at all North American locations. Smith and Barksdale participate in several of these interactive programs each year.

Surveys indicate that ninety percent of employees say the TV communication are useful to them in their work.

PUBLICATIONS ALSO HAVE HIGH PRIORITY

But publications also have a high priority at Federal Express, serving to supplement the TV programming and allowing for more comprehensive discussion of major developments and issues.

A quarterly *Worldwide* magazine goes to its 85,000 employees around the world. U.S. employees also receive a monthly Update newspaper plus a weekly bulletin board posting called This Week. In addition, special publications and videos go to targeted audiences such as couriers, pilots, aircraft mechanics and customer-service agents.

For its 5,000 managers, FedEx publishes *Manager's Pak,* a monthly packet of newspaper and magazine clippings.

BIG ROLE IN FLYING TIGERS MERGER

The advantages of having an operating satellite TV network were dramatized during the acquisition of the Flying Tigers organization by Federal Express during 1988–89. Martin said it helped to fill an urgent need to share information frequently with employees of both organizations.

FedEx's employee and management publications also carried major articles on the merger. But the major thrust of developments and plans was handled by satellite TV.

The process began on December 16, 1988, when plans were first announced through the FedEx satellite network at the same time the release was sent to external news media. Flying Tigers locations received tape versions of the announcement. Between then and the operational merger in August 1989, here is how Federal Express employees were kept up to date:

- Almost daily coverage on the morning news show.
- A weekly Monday update called "Joining Forces."
- Information was featured on company bulletin boards for employees who may have missed the TV update.
- Four live FXTV broadcasts during the 8-month merger period featured a number of top executives.

Flying Tigers employees also got priority attention through materials made available to all seventy FT locations, including videotapes of major programs carried live on FXTV, a special corporate video and a "Joining Forces" kit welcoming FT employees to Federal Express. This kit contained materials on company history, philosophy and business goals.

In April, a special videotape for FT employees was issued. It featured Smith and Barksdale in a Q&A format answering the most common questions being asked by FT employees and discussing their visions of business potential for the combined organization.

EXECUTIVE "TOWN MEETINGS"

In June, a series of "Town Meetings" took Smith, Barksdale and other top executives to the Los Angeles, New York and Columbus, Ohio areas where they talked to 2,000 of the 5,000 domestic Flying Tigers employees in a dozen meetings.

"Express Teams" of two to five FedEx employees also visited thirty of the largest Flying Tigers installations to distribute "welcome aboard" kits and answer questions.

On August 7, the day the merger was officially completed, FXTV broadcast merger news and commentary around the clock. By the end of 1989, three post-merger shows had been broadcast, discussing the significance of the merger and how the two organizations were being organized.

PROVIDED UNDERSTANDING AND ASSURANCE

Speaking of the experience, Martin says:

Our "Joining Forces" informational activities helped employees of both organizations better understand the reasons for the merger and gave them strong points for optimism and assurance about their own job security. Federal Express offered employment to all Flying Tigers, and the fact that eighty-nine percent agreed to stay was a very positive sign. Another important endorsement came when the combined pilot organization of about 2,000 voted 65–35 percent against representation by the Air Line Pilots Association (ALPA) even though the Flying Tigers pilot group of about a thousand had been previously represented by ALPA. Our frequent and open communication with employees made the transition a lot easier on everybody.

Our top executives support our communication efforts with more than words and dollars. In addition to easy accessibility, they stay actively involved in the overall communication through monthly editorial reviews. These meetings give us the opportunity to present our programs and plans and to discuss employee communication issues involved with upcoming management actions.

The continuous touch of our top executives strengthens their understanding and support for our total communication effort.

Chapter 9

Sell, Sell, Sell!
The Communicators Road
to Survival
and Success

"Sell, Sell, Sell!" is the title of a marvelous mini-film featuring Kermit the Frog telling in his own inimitable style how to succeed in business.

I've used part or all of this huckster show at least a dozen times in speeches.

Its message is absolutely true—performance plus salesmanship are the keys to an effective employee communication system. Neither can do it alone.

Good performance obviously is the number one goal for organizational communicators. But if you do an outstanding job yet hide your light under a basket, you may not get the recognition you deserve—or for that matter, the extra budget and people you need to get big things accomplished.

The truth is that being really successful in employee communication does require an aggressive, creative, many-faceted, continuing effort. You have to sell your program and let people know what it can do for the organization—in every niche, at every level, on every occasion. In contrast to more established activities, like media relations or advertising, the employee communication function in most organizations needs to be sold all the time.

CREATIVE, INNOVATIVE APPROACH NEEDED

Employee communication really lends itself to a strong, innovative approach. This is not to downgrade the importance of using proven methods of planning, research, salesmanship and implementation. But every organization is different in terms of what's needed, what will be accepted and what will be believed. Also, because it's still a relatively new professional field, one not yet fully accepted by many managements, it cries out for daring ideas and heavy merchandising to get its messages across and to win the attention of both employees and management alike. So, be an innovative communicator—find new and exciting ways of selling your program and ideas.

Union Carbide's Bob Berzok says:

> One of the most fundamental sales tools is the ability of the professional to demonstrate to management that employee communication can benefit the corporation's mission—if approached with candor, credibility, honesty and timeliness. Equally important is the recognition—by professionals and management alike—that the communication message, to be of value, must evoke an emotional response and appropriate action from employees.
>
> It is also important for professionals to have the ability to persuade, cajole, manipulate or convince senior management into recognizing the true power of communicating effectively with employees.

SOUND MANAGEMENT SYSTEMS GET PROPER RESPECT

Make sure your program is organized on a sound business basis, with special attention to planning, accountability and cost-effectiveness. Key management people need to know what is being achieved in employee communication, what major obstacles remain and what actions are being proposed to make further gains. And if you come up with excitingly different ways to move the program forward, that will add to its salability as well as its potential for success.

When you're looking for sales potential, think beyond the contributions that existing and proposed activities will make to your basic communication effort. Ask yourself whether you are making maximum use of these activities to sell the value of your program to management.

Here are some examples of key activities that represent sound management principles but also have important sales potential:

- Develop a strategic plan for employee communication strongly oriented to business goals—with the participation of key executives. An ounce of participation is worth a ton of communication.

- Establish a communication policy and guidelines for management, along with "information priorities." Astute strategic planning always impresses good managers.

- Establish a regular schedule of evaluation to audit strengths and weaknesses—and areas of new needs in employee communication. Make the communication function earn its keep, and make sure management knows it does.

Such activities will help convince key management people that the employee communication function is based on sound management and professional principles. These activities should be merchandised aggressively not only to top management but also throughout the organization, including to first-level supervisors when appropriate.

MANAGEMENT UPDATES AND INVOLVEMENT

Updates for managers will keep your program on the desks (and hopefully in the minds) of your managers on a regular basis. Here are some examples:

- *Presentations to top management.* Once a year presentations are a reasonable goal, but the results of a communication audit or a new strategic plan also are appropriate topics for additional presentations.

- *Written reports.* Sent to a broader spread of management people, they can report on major activities such as pilot projects, communication training seminars for managers or evaluations of representative plant publications.

An important avenue for selling is often overlooked—the direct involvement of key management people in as many communication activities as possible. Here are some examples:

- *Getting important executives involved.* They can be involved in the process of developing and updating communication plans and information priorities at both corporate and local levels.

- *Participation as speakers at communication conferences or seminars.* Special attention should be paid to "power spots" of the organization, such as financial, labor relations, strategic planning, marketing, product quality, legal and personnel.

- *Interviews.* Key executives can be used as the basis of special articles in publications or visual presentations for employees.

Respect from managers is an extremely valuable sales asset. But so is understanding and recognition from employees. A corporate-wide employee communication program needs respect and recognition, not just at the corporate level but also at local levels throughout the company.

Communicators also should be constantly seeking other opportunities to sell management and employees on the importance of their communication activities, in working toward the achievement of organizational goals.

Some of us have had the opportunity of starting from scratch with a charter for establishing a company-wide employee communication system; and it's a great feeling knowing that whatever you do, it's going to be infinitely better than what was there before. But you also have an obligation to bring the entire organization up to a level of effectiveness which equals (or exceeds) that of your major competitors—and to do it as quickly as possible.

SELLING CAMPAIGNS

One technique that can provide a solid base of ownership and support from the manager group is to conduct a selling campaign covering all major locations. Ideally, such a campaign should be preceded by a comprehensive audit and an action plan based on the findings. This selling campaign might involve development of a slide or videotape presentation for local management, one which outlines the philosophy, goals and major elements of the company employee communication program, including services available to local units.

Most of these presentations could be given by members of the corporate employee communication staff, followed by question-and-answer sessions. However, enlisting the help of other company public relations or personnel executives could spread the work load and strengthen the base of understanding and support for employee communication.

A campaign of this type could be conducted every few years to bring local management and communication professionals up to date and to solicit suggestions for strengthening the corporate program and also services to local units.

PILOT PROJECTS HAVE HIGH POTENTIAL

Use of the pilot-project concept is another high-potential idea for multi-location organizations. The idea would be to establish "ideal" communication systems at two or more different facilities. Use of "control" facilities which would establish no changes in their normal activities might be desirable to produce comparable improvement data. On the other hand, you might want to forget the comparison game and simply go 100 percent at all locations, trying different concepts and ideas to see what works best. Highly important, a corporate effort should be organized to take full advantage of lessons learned in the program.

That's what General Motors did in the 1983–88 period, constructing what they called an "idea factory," which systematically shared new and different approaches with all other operations across the corporation. (See Case Example 10 at the end of this chapter on pages 221-24.)

USE EXISTING ACTIVITIES TO SELL TOTAL PROGRAM

It's sometimes easy to become so involved with establishing a new program, or carrying out a regular part of an existing communication effort, that we neglect to take advantage of its selling value. Here are some examples of major activities and the kind of selling potential they represent:

Communication Audits

Three comprehensive communication audits conducted by General Motors in the 1982–86 period produced valuable information and guidance for improving the entire communication system. But they also provided the opportunity to involve a large number of managers and employees and to sell them on the concepts and goals of the communication effort. Here's how:

- Twenty-eight plants or staffs were directly involved in the studies, with 6,000 employees completing surveys. Presentations highlighting its own survey results were made to management at most of these locations by local communication managers.

- Twenty plants and about 600 employees took part in the focus-group discussions which preceded the surveys.

- More than seventy top corporate, divisional and plant executives were interviewed for ideas and suggestions.

- Broad distribution of the results and recommendations was made to management throughout the corporation.

- Results also were covered in management and employee communication media at both the corporate and local levels; those plants and staffs which participated in the studies were given special emphasis.

In total, more than forty plants, 650 managers and 6,000 employees were directly involved in the communication process and had the opportunity to give their input.

These audits—and the full exploitation of the results in follow-up publicity and selling activities—were a major plus in advancing the total employee communication system.

Similar "merchandising" benefits were secured by Weyerhaeuser Paper Company in its 1987 communication audit, which involved thirty-one executive interviews and 800 employees participating in focus-group discussions at twenty-six of the company's U.S. locations. Aggressive selling before and after the study provided a solid foundation of support for development of an effective company-wide communication system.

Communication Training for Managers

A series of two-day communication training seminars, which were conducted in 1984 for 230 General Motors plant managers by Communispond, Inc., were largely devoted to skills training.

A special sales orientation was included. More than 2 hours were devoted to explaining the important role of managers in the total communication process and to discussing practical, in-plant communication problems and solutions.

A higher level of salesmanship was involved in a more advanced one-day training seminar, one which was organized by GM in 1986 with the help of Roger D'Aprix, then with Towers, Perrin, Forster and Crosby. The main purposes were to convey basic concepts of organizational communication and to advise managers on how to apply them to their own communication problems back home. More than 1,000 managers participated in seminar sessions during the 1986–88 period.

These two series of seminars probably did more to boost the recognition of and respect for employee communication in General Motors than any other single activity during the 1984–88 period. They spotlighted the plant manager (or equivalent administrative manager) as the key to effective communication and also worked to improve his or her skills and confidence.

Even more significantly, the seeds of potential which were planted in these seminars will continue to bear fruit as many of the participants assume management jobs of increasing importance in the years ahead.

Communicators' Conferences

The traditional communicators' conference involves a meeting of company publication editors or communicators from staffs and outlying locations, one designed to teach such basics as content, writing, editing, layout and approvals. Add a speech or two by corporate executives and you have a pretty solid two-day agenda.

But if your conference only satisfies the needs for training and on-site information sharing with low- or mid-level company officials, you're missing a boatload of opportunities for advancing the total communication effort. Here are some major selling points:

- Ideally, let's say you have just finished a communication study which spotlighted what business issues top the priority lists of both employees and managers. Select the top five or six issues. These will make up the core content for the conference, and they will also determine what executives will be invited to participate.

Selling Point: Professional research is important; it commands appropriate action involving all of the company's communicators. The study has pointed out the most critical business issues as determined by the opinions of both employees and managers.

- Secure the company's top executives responsible for the subjects on your agenda—including either the chairman or president—to make presentations and conduct candid question-and-answer sessions.

Selling Point: A number of top company executives get personally involved in your program, and they provide substance, authority, prestige and significance to the conference. It's something editors can take home and talk about with their bosses to encourage their support.

- For the training aspects, recruit the best editors and communicators from your company to direct these sessions; also go outside for a top consultant or an expert from another company, someone with an outstanding communication record.

Selling Point: Broad involvement of top company professional talent leads to sharing of ideas and experience, prestige, and teamwork among communicators.

- Even while the conference is going on, prepare a newsletter-type publication with highlights of the conference which can be distributed to all company communicators as well as to the total management group. Promptness in getting this out to the troops is important; strike while the iron is hot.

Selling Point: Conference information can be spread to all employees through local communication activities. Management people can share the conference experience and gain a better appreciation of the high level of professionalism incorporated in your whole program.

By embodying the research results, by achieving strong management participation and by infusing a professional orientation into the communication job, a communicators' conference can be a valuable selling tool for the total communication system.

IN-HOUSE CONSULTING SERVICES

Offering an in-house consulting service in employee communication is an effective means of strengthening local activities through work with local management and communication professionals. If done properly on a continuing basis, over a period of time, the cumulative effects can be substantial.

Preparation of a special presentation, which can be given formally with slides or informally around a conference table, can be of great help in explaining basic concepts, what good communication can do for the organization, and what services are available from company headquarters. Ideally, the initial meeting at each location would include the plant manager and his or her staff (including the communicator); and if the program goes well, a much larger group could be included on later visits.

Many of the managers who benefit from counseling services become strong advocates and lend personal support to the communication effort in a variety of ways. For example, they might be willing to participate in communication events, pilot projects, audits and focus-group discussions, just to name a few. Each successful consulting experience helps to increase the field strength and overall stature of the corporate communication effort—in addition to benefiting the local program as well.

Equally important, consulting services provide a vital pipeline to the frontlines of the business, producing a two-way exchange of information and ideas. This helps keep field managers up-to-date on services available; it also keeps corporate communication people wired into field needs—as well as providing firsthand reactions and suggestions concerning corporate activities.

Dan Koger, of TPF&C, is a strong advocate of in-house counseling as a means for building a strong foundation and durability into employee communication systems. He used results of a comprehensive audit, done when he was with Weyerhaeuser Paper Company, as the basis for an aggressive program of consulting with local managers.

IDEAS FROM OTHER ORGANIZATIONS

Another technique which has been very effective in my own work over the years has been the study of how comparable organizations handle a particular problem. As the old saying goes: "Steal good ideas wherever you can find them."

Most companies are usually cooperative in providing basic information about their pet projects by mail; and within reason, they will grant interviews to fellow professionals either in person or over the telephone. Active participation in professional organizations can also provide useful information about how others have attacked thorny problems with success. Higher-level executives are usually more impressed with a new proposal if they know that other well-known firms have similar activities which are producing good results in attacking common problems.

PROFIT FROM YOUR CRISES

Communication managers at companies that go through crisis situations should make the most of their bruises to build a stronger communication program once the storms have passed. Profit from your pain.

Unfortunately, the most comfortable thing to do is to wipe off the cold sweat and let the crisis slowly become just an unpleasant memory. The truth is that you'll probably never find your top management more receptive about upgrading your program than in the immediate post-crisis period.

Strike while management can still feel the pain—inflicted perhaps as a result of stockholder, employee or public rebuke. Crisis plans are not the answer; an effective on-going, credible communication system is.

Tell your management people what your program needs in order to be first-class. Tell them what is needed to build an employee base of trust and confidence on a year-round basis; the goal is to create a climate of goodwill so employees will believe top management if another hurricane hits.

Done promptly, a post-crisis improvement plan can be a very effective selling vehicle for advancing your total employee communication system on an enduring basis.

"OUTSIDE" COUNSELORS

Don't be afraid to use outside consultants to help sell the communication program to top management.

Consultants bring a valuable synergistic viewpoint to the corporate boardroom—a collective experience gained through similar projects done with other companies. And management people are almost always more impressed by outside experts than by those in their own companies.

But don't expect outside consultants to perform miracles—at least not without a lot of help from the company's communication staff.

The counselors' biggest disadvantage is that they don't know the company, its built-in biases and blind spots or where the political power lies. They may not know what will be interpreted as "acceptable, constructive advice" from outsiders and what will be viewed as naive or pretentious.

Sometimes the overpuff, sugar coatings and distortions of truth go so far they border on dishonesty.

Be careful of overpuff from outside counselors. One reason for hiring outside experts is the hope that they can find different ways of telling your story more favorably. But sometimes the overpuff, sugar coatings and distortions of truth go so far that they border on dishonesty.

This happened to us once when a consultant rewrote a videotape script of highlights from a GM conference for financial analysts; this videotape program had been designed for use for our total management group. In essence, the rewrite said that "everything was coming up roses in GM." That simply was not true—as most of the intended audience knew only too well—because most of the hard remedies were in their laps. Fortunately, the proposed script never got past public relations or personnel people—so a credibility disaster was avoided.

Working with an outside consultant requires a lot of teamwork and sharing of confidential information, some of it very personal in nature. Sharing and trust are essential.

Outside experts can provide a measure of support and credibility sometimes unattainable by inside experts, however good they may be. They represent extra firepower, not only in strengthening your program but also in selling it to top management.

SUMMARY

Countless opportunities are available for keeping management at all levels aware of your program and for selling its value to the performance and morale of both employees and managers.

Let no opportunity escape. Large or small, recognize it not only as good management practice but also as a day-by-day process of survival, recognition and success for your function and for you.

Be innovative in adapting tried-and-true concepts and techniques. Be constantly on the lookout for better, more exciting ways of getting your messages across, directing attention to your programs and encouraging support and participation of both management and employees alike.

CASE 12

General Motors Corporation

AN IDEA FACTORY
FOR A CORPORATE-WIDE
EMPLOYEE COMMUNICATION SYSTEM

In 1983, General Motors employee communication people took what appeared to be a bad suggestion from a member of top management and turned it into a tremendous asset for the corporation's employee communication system.

TASK FORCE REPORT

It happened at a meeting of top corporate management, where the employee communication section had presented a "task force" report recommending substantial increases in both manpower and budgets for upgrading corporate-wide communication efforts. One proposal was to add the equivalent of 100 people and increase annual expenditures for publications by $5 to $10 million.

While the executives accepted the need to improve communication and supported the proposed corporate concept, they didn't want to mandate such changes to the divisions. They recommended two things: (1) more aggressive selling to the company's divisions—with visible top management support, and (2) the institution of a pilot program to be sure we had the right formula for state-of-the-art communication systems.

The employee communication group agreed with the proposal to put on a corporate-wide selling campaign to encourage divisions to beef up their communication activities. But it wanted no part of a "pilot program" which would delay further development of the total corporate system for 2 or 3 years while trying to prove its people knew what they were doing.

So, the employee communication group decided to launch a "Leadership Project" rather than a pilot. Instead of two control and two pilot plants, all four plants would go all out with the most advanced thinking and techniques, with adequate staff, budget and management support.

Directing the project was Bruce McCristal, who was GM's director of employee communications and is now public affairs director of GM Hughes Electronics.

KEY ELEMENTS

It is interesting in retrospect to examine the nine key elements established in early 1983 for the plants selected for the leadership project:

1. An initial benchmark survey to evaluate current systems and deficiencies.
2. A written communication plan, with the participation of and approval by top unit management.
3. A qualified full-time communication manager, reporting directly to the unit manager. In view of the austerity climate of that time, this was the toughest requirement, but locations had to make this commitment to be included in the program.
4. A publications program, involving at minimum, a newsletter three times a week plus a bimonthly tabloid with content heavily oriented toward business goals.
5. State-of-the-business meetings for all employees to be held at least twice a year, and involving participation by union leadership if possible.
6. Daily electronic or telephone newslines.
7. Upward communication, including face-to-face meetings by top unit managers with supervisors and employees.
8. For supervisors, a regular pipeline of information from corporate and local sources—also communication skills training.
9. Periodic professional evaluations of progress.

Anyone designing a new employee communication plan today would find these elements an excellent starting point.

HEAVY DEMAND FOR PARTICIPATION

After initial progress was reported back to GM's public relations policy group, there was a flurry of demand from other locations to be part of the project. Almost overnight, fifteen divisions or plants were involved. Although it taxed corporate staff resources to provide the selling, coordinating and study activities involved, the project was viewed with great optimism and given a number one priority.

Corporate staff members made presentations to top management at most of the fifteen locations over a 3-month start-up period. Involvement of local union leadership was strongly encouraged, as was discussion of the project in various employee communication media. It was a project which was based on certain proven fundamentals but which also encouraged innovative approaches to tailor specific communication programs for each participating organization.

It was easy to garner enthusiastic support at divisional and plant levels early in the project when top corporate endorsement—in the form of executive memos to the field—was obvious and repeated. Unfortunately, once the "roman candle" effect of strong corporate backing subsided, so did the energies which some of the locations gave to the expanded communication efforts.

Extensive cost-cutting efforts across the corporation squeezed out both full-time professionals and funds at some locations. The biggest flaw in the entire project was the inability of locations to find qualified professionals within their own organizations—or at other GM units—and hiring from outside GM was virtually impossible because of austerity restrictions. Transfers of strong managers, who were strong communication advocates, to other responsibilities also hurt.

SUCCESSFUL IMPACT ON TOTAL SYSTEM

The program operated as a Leadership Project officially for more than three years. Significant improvements were achieved—and lessons were learned—at most locations.

Idea sharing among the fifteen locations was a priority goal from the beginning—and this was done largely at monthly meetings in Detroit. The fifteen locations discussed their experiments and new approaches—what worked best, what didn't and why. Employee communication directors from other companies also were invited to make presentations of their own outstanding activities.

As the program developed, it was obvious that much greater benefits could be secured by sharing the resulting good ideas with communicators and managers across the corporation. In 1984, the monthly meetings were opened to representatives of any GM location—whether officially in the project or not—and attendance more than doubled. These meetings were continued, although less frequently, for 2 years after the Leadership Project officially ended.

Reports on these activities were covered in *Communication Ideas,* a monthly newsletter for about 1,000 managers and communicators. And a

30-minute videotape, which was entitled "Communicating for Performance" and which featured six outstanding locations, was produced for managers and communicators.

SUMMARY

As McCristal says:

> The Leadership Project was an "idea factory" for a sizable share of GM locations, providing regular reports on new techniques, approaches and unusual experiences in the communication field. It was a valuable vehicle for selling a modern communication process. It stirred competition and spotlighted achievements in improving the level of communication across GM. It emphasized the importance of custom designing local programs to fit the local environment and communication needs. The project had an extra measure of credibility because of its "top management mandate" and also because it involved so many respected locations and people in those organizations.

The Leadership Project paid off in spades—not only in advancing the corporate-wide communication system professionally but also in helping to convince a broad segment of General Motors management of the fundamental importance of communication in the management process.

Chapter 10

Conclusions
and
A Look Ahead

The 1980s brought revolutionary changes to the American business and industrial work place, alterations which have had a profound— and to a large degree negative—effect on management-employee relations. And the reverberations of these changes are producing similar modifications in other private and public institutions as well.

Mergers, leveraged buyouts, acquisitions, downsizing, joint ventures with foreign firms and total reorganizations are symbols of the thrashing dynamics of change. Massive reorientations of organizations have occurred—or are still in progress—involving the fundamental structure, culture, products, technology and management styles of many major institutions. And changes in careers and life patterns of employees have been a core part of the industrial transformation process.

None of these changes has been more massive than those experienced by companies like General Motors and AT&T. But for a much broader spectrum of private and public institutions in this country, basic management-employee relationships, involving qualities such as loyalty, commitment, trust and confidence, will never be the same. This represents a management challenge of the highest magnitude—one in which effective communication has a special responsibility.

NEW AWARENESS OF EMPLOYEE VALUE FOR SUCCESS

There is a healthy new awareness among leaders of American business and industry that people do have a value for success "above everything else." And substantial efforts are being made by some companies to develop new philosophies and new work environments which give greater attention to the concerns, aspirations, creativity and potential of all employees—both as individuals and in teams.

In the final analysis, it is people who will make the difference over time. And the more progressive leaders of American institutions are now searching for new management concepts that will regenerate human resources in positive ways for the twenty-first century.

As management guru Peter Drucker says in *Time,* "We are already in the new century…, [but] many are still stuck in the world of 1960. What we face now is totally new and dynamic—and we are quite unprepared for it."

GLOBAL PERSPECTIVE AND CHANGING PRIORITIES

As communicators, we must guard against being too insular and short-sighted in our thinking—about our companies and our profession. In most business concerns, this means adopting a more global perspective in assessing organizational goals and problems in a world arena that will be even more competitive.

On a worldwide basis, for example, dramatic changes in the political/economic/military goals of nations in Europe and Asia forecast dynamic potential in economic and consumer demands for hundreds of millions of people. On a national basis, it also means being more conscious of changing priorities of our own country, changes that require extra study and planning *now* for those who would be leaders tomorrow.

Military defense is a good case in point. This subject has been a national and world preoccupation for the last half century. But changing world politics indicate that the next decade will probably see a lessening of defense pressures, with concerns about the physical environment and human needs in most of the world moving to center stage. These trends will have significant effects on such key areas as research and development, new products, financial outlays for air and water pollution control, as well as energy use.

OTHER TRENDS SHAPING THE COMMUNICATION FUNCTION

These changing priorities have direct effects on the substance and emphasis of communication in American institutions—with both external and internal audiences.

Greater efforts will go toward achieving more cohesion in managing and understanding global operations. Corporate control will be further decentralized. There will be increasing emphasis on value measurement of all company activities, including internal and external communications. Special incentives at all levels will encourage and reward performance above and beyond normal requirements.

We can also expect increasingly strong actions by business management to bring about more cooperative, participative, trusting relations with employees and unions. Intensified efforts will be needed for control of substance abuse in the work place, predicted by some to be "a battleground for drugs" in the 1990s.

Other pressures for change will come from an exploding retiree population and from demands for equal opportunity for all employees in all aspects of the work place.

With respect to media, look for greater emphasis on face-to-face activities and for much broader use of television—particularly satellite TV—in internal communication. Television should play a particularly significant role in the larger, geographically-dispersed organizations and in the sharing of varied business information with managers.

Viewed in the perspective of these kinds of challenges, there are even more reasons why an investment in better communication with employees is good business.

A well-directed employee communication program represents a fundamental management resource with a tremendous untapped potential for helping American business become number one again all over the world. It can help to build more cooperative relationships among management, unions and employees. Likewise, it can help to improve overall employee performance, attitudes and teamwork in any type of organization—including those in business, government, and education, as well as in health, church, community and other service areas.

EMPLOYEES STILL TAKEN FOR GRANTED

But to be most effective in improving communication systems, we must begin with the cliché that people really are our most important asset and therefore must rate top priority in terms of communication. In many companies, however, top management has to alter its thinking to validate this assumption.

In many organizations, employees have been—and still are—taken for granted. At the very least, they are ranked on the communication ladder behind the news media, stockholders, financial analysts and politicians.

This is shabby treatment, indeed, for the people who make the organization go. For it is employees on whom the organization depends for volume, quality and efficiency in all its operations. And it is employees on whom the organization depends for loyalty to company products and support against unfair government regulations—just to name a few of the expectations management has of its employees.

So, how do companies motivate people to become more committed to top performance, loyalty and pride in their work; to reach back for that extra effort that turns ordinary workers into committed team members?

Obviously, tough authoritative managers aren't the answer. But old management habits are hard to break and stubborn vestiges of archaism remain in some places.

Higher wages and benefits also have lost their luster with the new generation of employees who choose to spend more time with their families and on recreation, and who seek more participation, decision-making responsibilities and personal gratification in their work.

Today's employees seek greater control over their own work destinies in return for higher levels of performance and commitment. There is without question a strong momentum for greater democracy in the workplace—and there is tremendous potential for the organizations that recognize and respond constructively to these demands.

NEW BIBLE FOR MANAGEMENT-EMPLOYEE RELATIONS

There is a new bible for management-employee relations—and it offers great potential for all kinds of organizations, large and small.

It talks about management having respect for employees and their opinions and ideas, about sharing, trust and caring for employees as individuals. It doesn't ask managers to be soft or to coddle poor performers. Rather, it calls for a demanding and challenging partnership that generates enthusiasm and pride among employees in doing a better job.

In some respects, the answer seems as simple as a few bible-like parables, such as: caring begets caring, sharing begets sharing, give and you shall receive.

CONTRIBUTIONS EMPLOYEE COMMUNICATION CAN MAKE

So what can better communication contribute as a chapter in the new bible on management-employee relations? What can employee communication do to help top executives achieve greater productivity, harmony and job satisfaction in working together with their employees? Here are some examples of what such a program can do. It can:

- Create a climate for open communication that stimulates new and different ideas by encouraging candid criticism without fear of retribution.

- Help employees become more informed about the business, so they understand it and its leaders better.

- Help to motivate employees to come to work every day, to produce quality products or service and to give top performance on their jobs—and to understand why their own family security depends on it.

- Make it easier for people to accept tough decisions because they have been given the reasons why.

- Make employees feel like full-fledged members of the team, by trusting them with key business information and empowering them to make decisions about activities that affect their jobs; and it makes them feel that their individual and group efforts are important to the company's success.

- Instill in employees a feeling of pride, confidence and commitment because they know so much about the organization, its plans and aspirations—and because they know they are an important part of it all.

- Inform employees about public issues so they can make considered judgments concerning the company's views, allowing them to be knowledgeable, participating citizens.

- Engage the brain power of all employees by listening to their ideas and encouraging them to reach out more and more.

These are major reasons why investment in employee communication has so much potential. Good communication does earn its keep. But the employee communication function needs support and recognition if it is to carry out its responsibilities at the highest levels of performance.

THE "SOUL" OF EMPLOYEE COMMUNICATION

In the new bible of management-employee relations, in addition to the chapter on people, there is one devoted to the "soul" of employee communication—the management philosophy under which it operates best.

It begins with the premise that employee communication is a legitimate and necessary management function in all types of modern organizations and should rank in importance at least on a par with labor relations, news relations, personnel and other key staff functions.

Top management must declare and define this higher level of responsibility by establishing policies and guidelines and by continuing to support employee communication activities. The employee communication director must have access to high-level company information and must be called upon regularly to counsel management on all matters of direct interest to employees that will involve communication. Without strong management support—by rules and by example—the function will wither and die.

MISSION OF EMPLOYEE COMMUNICATION

The overriding mission of the employee communication function is to carry out open, honest information sharing with employees while serving as a strong advocate for management thinking and actions. Its operations should be based on short- and long-range plans developed strongly around business goals and employee needs as expressed through research, discussions and regular access to important company information.

The employee communication function serves as an important link between management and employees, and this represents not only a management responsibility but an obligation of trust to employees as well. Employee communication professionals should oppose any actions by unions, government or anyone else that would restrict, distort or curtail management's obligation to communicate fully, on a regular basis, with its employees about all aspects of the business.

Employee communication managers should be aggressive in promoting healthy two-way communication between management and employees, between corporate and field management, and between management and the unions. The creation of a permissive atmosphere for upward communication is essential, one which encourages criticism of all aspects of the work place as a basis for doing a better job and making work more enjoyable.

The management organization and communication are like the cardiovascular system of the human body. The management organization is the prime top-to-bottom link with employees. It represents the network of arteries which holds the corporate body together. And communication is the lifeblood which draws its informational strength from various sources, recasts it into digestible forms and transmits the revitalized materials to every part of the corporate body.

If the power from the heart isn't strong enough to drive energies to every extremity, they will cease to function and become dead weight on the total corporate body. And if there's no flow back to the heart of the organization, the body will atrophy and die.

CLOSER TIES BETWEEN COMMUNICATORS AND MANAGERS

That is why, if the communication system is to be a vital force, all managers must accept a prime responsibility for communicating with employees—in order to advance their own managerial capabilities and to enhance employee understanding, trust, teamwork and performance.

Professional communicators—whether in headquarters or in outlying factories, warehouses or sales offices—have a key role in helping managers to communicate more effectively and to build a strong communication network.

The most successful communicators are those who think like managers. And the best managers are those who think and act like professional communicators.

Operating from the manager's viewpoint can help to eliminate the criticism which some executives level at communicators: that they do not understand the complexities of managing the business or the serious business risks sometimes involved in the communication process. Viewing the communication function through the eyes of managers also will help communicators in developing diversified plans in sync with operating goals and with higher leadership aspirations.

This is why content is so important. It's the hard stuff which gives practical purpose to communication priorities—particularly at local levels. And discussing both sides of controversial issues allows employees to make better judgments and to feel more like full-fledged members of the team.

In seeking continuous improvements in performance, communication managers have an obligation to experiment and try new approaches. Creativity, imagination and risk taking are vital. Cutting a new trail or pushing out beyond safe waters is simply a part of selling new ideas, of getting better every day. The employee communication function also must carry out regular professional evaluations to measure progress—and to modify and strengthen activities based on these evaluations.

The role of employee communication in the management structure of business—and in other public and private institutions as well—has grown tremendously in the past decade or so in terms of opportunities, performance and respect. We must recognize, however, that most of these advances have come not in seven-league steps but usually one step at a time—often with two steps forward and one backwards.

Gains are often transitory if they are not institutionalized; they can fade away or regress with new management or with less committed communication managers, or if economics or politics move to center stage. That's the nature of progress in virgin forests where ignorance, politics and tradition would have you go the other way— or simply go away.

FULFILLING THE POTENTIAL OF EMPLOYEE COMMUNICATION

Fulfilling the ultimate potential of employee communication as a valued member of the management function will depend on a number of factors:

- Management must recognize the critical need for demonstrating with action that employees *are* the organization's most important public; that management sincerely cares about them as individuals as well as workers; and that honest, open, two-way communication is an integral part of a healthy, productive management-employee relationship. Only then will the full potential of teamwork, technology and people be reflected in maximum performance gains—along with higher levels of employee satisfaction and rewards.

Management should replace politics, territorial jealousies and power struggles with a unified communication effort.

- Management should direct special attention to eliminating in-house obstacles to open communication—by replacing politics, territorial jealousies and power struggles with a unified communication effort to maximize employee understanding and support.

- Communication should be an integral part of the appraisal and reward systems for managers at every level, and ways must be found to measure these objectively in line with responsibilities. Actions speak louder than words.

- Top management, public relations and personnel executives should work together to establish appropriate recruitment activities, career paths and reward incentives to help make employee communication an attractive career field from entry level through top executive positions.

- Professional societies should continue to offer quality training and other services covering the wide range of careers in this field, staying abreast of an ever-changing and increasingly demanding profession.

- Colleges and universities should devote more attention to this career field. It is estimated that as many as 200,000 people are employed in various public relations jobs in business, government, medicine, religion and other service organizations in the United States—with an increasing share employed in employee communication. Universities must do a better job of tailoring curricula to practical requirements of the employee communication field, and of broadening internship training for both professors and students.

- More effective research tools and methodologies require the best efforts of professional societies and universities as well as of private and public institutions. Of particular importance is the need to define, in quantitative as well as in qualitative terms, the value of communication in achieving organizational goals.

WHAT COMMUNICATORS MUST DO

Some internal communicators feel they represent, at their best, the conscience of their organizations; they are the warriors who fight for the whole truth and for real-life responses to legitimate employee information needs.

The mission of our profession often goes against the grain of tradition and autocracy. It is our responsibility to communicate as much business information as possible without harming the company—despite many who still believe we should communicate as little as necessary.

Yet, this is where employee communicators can do the most good for their organizations:

- By spending more effort in interpreting and explaining management actions to employees so they are better understood and accepted.

- By zeroing in on the major short- and long-term goals of the organization to achieve maximum purpose, continuity and value for the total internal communication effort.

- By providing more information and support services to help all managers become better communicators.

In so doing, management respect and integrity will be enhanced, as will the magnitude of contributions which the employee communication function can make.

This will be the decade of the employee; and it will also be the decade of the innovative communicator. The tremendous potential of this powerful human resource can no longer be ignored or recognized half-heartedly. Good, honest interactive communication is vital to all of our hoped for performance and progress. But realization of its full potential will require aggressive, innovative approaches to construct strong new, trusting kinds of partnership between managers and employees to drive all of our enterprises forward to new heights.

In the final analysis, employee communication professionals themselves will have the biggest say in determining what levels of recognition, responsibility and rewards will be accorded this important activity. It is essentially a matter of earning—through outstanding, ethical performance—those levels of achievement, respect and integrity which this profession deserves.

Index